LEARN TO
Knit in the Round

Ridged Mobius, page 32

www.companyscoming.com
visit our website

Rolled–Brim Hat & Mitts, page 81

Learn to Knit in the Round

First Printing November 2009

Library and Archives Canada Cataloguing in Publication
Learn to knit in the round.
(Company's Coming crafts)
Includes index.
ISBN 978-1-897477-21-2
1. Knitting--Technique. 2. Knitting--Patterns. I. Title: Knit in the round. II. Series: Company's coming crafts
TT820.L435 2009   746.43'2028   C2009-901336-3

Published by
Company's Coming Publishing Limited
2311-96 Street
Edmonton, Alberta, Canada T6N 1G3
Tel: 780-450-6223 Fax: 780-450-1857
www.companyscoming.com

Company's Coming is a registered trademark owned by Company's Coming Publishing Limited

Printed in China

The Company's Coming Story

Jean Paré grew up with an understanding that family, friends and home cooking are the key ingredients for a good life. A mother of four, Jean worked as a professional caterer for 18 years, operating out of her home kitchen. During that time, she came to appreciate quick and easy recipes that call for everyday ingredients. In answer to mounting requests for her recipes, Company's Coming cookbooks were born, and Jean moved on to a new chapter in her career.

Company's Coming founder Jean Paré

Just as Company's Coming continues to promote the tradition of home cooking, the same is now true with crafting. Like good cooking, great craft results depend upon easy-to-follow instructions, readily available materials and enticing photographs of the finished products. Also like cooking, crafting is meant to be enjoyed in the home or cottage. Company's Coming Crafts, then, is a natural extension from the kitchen into the family room or den.

In the beginning, Jean worked from a spare bedroom in her home, located in the small prairie town of Vermilion, Alberta, Canada. The first Company's Coming cookbook, *150 Delicious Squares*, was an immediate bestseller. Today, with well over 150 titles in print, Company's Coming has earned the distinction of publishing Canada's most popular cookbooks. The company continues to gain new supporters by adhering to Jean's "Golden Rule of Cooking"—Never share a recipe you wouldn't use yourself. It's an approach that has worked—millions of times over!

Company's Coming cookbooks are distributed throughout Canada, the United States, Australia and other international English-language markets. French and Spanish language editions have also been published. Sales to date have surpassed 25 million copies with no end in sight. Familiar and trusted in home kitchens around the world, Company's Coming cookbooks are highly regarded both as kitchen workbooks and as family heirlooms.

Because Company's Coming operates a test kitchen and not a craft shop, we've partnered with a major North American craft content publisher to assemble a variety of craft compilations exclusively for us. Our editors have been involved every step of the way. You can see the excellent results for yourself in the book you're holding.

Company's Coming Crafts are for everyone—whether you're a beginner or a seasoned pro. What better gift could you offer than something you've made yourself? In these hectic days, people still enjoy crafting parties; they bring family and friends together in the same way a good meal does. Company's Coming is proud to support crafters with this new creative book series.

We hope you enjoy these easy-to-follow, informative and colourful books, and that they inspire your creativity. So, don't delay—get crafty!

TABLE OF CONTENTS

Sweaters & Wraps

Step out in style in sweaters and wraps that are knit in the round.

Babies & Kids

Soft and sweet like the little ones in your life, these garments will be a joy to knit.

Dot & Dash Pullover, page 40

Icy Blue Shell, page 37

Little Miss Precious, page 64

TABLE OF CONTENTS

Hats & Mittens

For a weekend of fun knitting,
make one of these colourful
cold-weather accessories.

Socks & Sundry

These cozy knitted socks and
unique projects are great
for crafters on the go.

Crisscross Cable Glass Cozy, page 114

Silly Hat, page 97

Pretty Stripe Socks, page 107

Feeling Crafty? Get Creative!

Each 160-page book features easy-to-follow, step-by-step instructions and full-page colour photographs of every project. Whatever your crafting fancy, there's a Company's Coming Creative Series craft book to match!

Beading: Beautiful Accessories in Under an Hour
Complement your wardrobe, give your home extra flair or add an extra-special personal touch to gifts with these quick and easy beading projects. Create any one of these special crafts in an hour or less.

Knitting: Easy Fun for Everyone
Take a couple of needles and some yarn and see what beautiful things you can make! Learn how to make fashionable sweaters, comfy knitted blankets, scarves, bags and other knitted crafts with these easy-to-intermediate knitting patterns.

Card Making: Handmade Greetings for All Occasions
Making your own cards is a fun, creative and inexpensive way of letting someone know you care. Stamp, emboss, quill or layer designs in a creative and unique card with your own personal message for friends or family.

Patchwork Quilting
In this book full of throws, baby quilts, table toppers, wall hangings—and more—you'll find plenty of beautiful projects to try. With the modern fabrics available, and the many practical and decorative applications, patchwork quilting is not just for Grandma!

Crocheting: Easy Blankets, Throws & Wraps
Find projects perfect for decorating your home, for looking great while staying warm or for giving that one-of-a-kind gift. A range of simple but stunning designs make crocheting quick, easy and entertaining.

Sewing: Fun Weekend Projects
Find a wide assortment of easy and attractive projects to help you create practical storage solutions, decorations for any room or just the right gift for that someone special. Create table runners, placemats, baby quilts, pillows and more!

For more information about Company's Coming craft books, visit our website, www.companyscoming.com

FOREWORD

In this book, you will learn to use circular needles and double-pointed needles or learn to use them better. There are step-by-step instructions to follow for those who haven't used these needles before. All the patterns in this book use circular or double-pointed needles, so you will have plenty of occasions to practice.

At one time, these needles were only used by experienced knitters when the pattern design required them. That is not true today! Just as knitters have discovered, you, too, will find that knitting in the round is very easy. It doesn't require years of knitting experience. Today many experienced knitters use circular needles whenever possible because they are lighter in weight and available in many different finishes. Many new knitters are also finding circular needles, and even double-pointed needles, easy to use. Of course, everyone loves having fewer seams to sew at the end!

Even if you're just learning to knit, there isn't a better way to spend a weekend than knitting for a sweet new baby or special youngster in your life. Choose colours and yarns that kids love to create the perfect top or snuggly bunting. With projects ranging from beginner to intermediate levels, the Babies & Kids chapter is sure to be a favourite.

You can step out in style in a lovely hand-knit project from the Sweaters & Wraps chapter. Use chunky yarn and big needles to create the Yukon Pullover, or choose a cotton-blend yarn for the lovely, light-weight Icy Blue Shell. To keep you looking good from head to toe, try your hand at stylish hats, mittens and socks to add the perfect finishing touch to your outfit. The Hats & Mittens chapter includes page after page of fashionable projects.

The last chapter of the book, Socks & Sundry, features fun, one-of-a-kind projects that make unique gifts to share with your friends and family. You'll want to make one of each to keep for yourself as well. As mentioned above, all projects are knit on double-pointed or circular needles or both. Prepare yourself to be amazed at how easy it is to use circular or double-pointed needles.

The skills that you learn in this book will carry you through a lifetime of knitting enjoyment, and the projects are sure to please. Come on now, let's get started!

Slumber Party Sleeping Bag, page 120

KNITTING BASICS

Getting Started

Supplies Needed for Practice Lessons:

One 3½ oz skein of knitting worsted weight yarn in a
   light colour
Size 8 (5mm) 10-inch long straight knitting needles
Size H/8/5mm crochet hook (for repairs)
Scissors
Tape measure
Size 16 tapestry needle or plastic yarn needle

To knit, you need only a pair of knitting needles, some
yarn, a pair of scissors, a tape measure, a crochet hook and
a tapestry or yarn needle. Later on, for some of the projects
in this book, you can add all kinds of accessories such as
markers, stitch holders and needle point protectors. But for
now, you only need the items listed above.

Yarn

Yarn comes in a wonderful selection of fibres, ranging
from wool to metallic; textures from lumpy to smooth;
colours from the palest pastels to vibrant neon shades;
and weights from gossamer fine to chunky.

The most commonly used yarn, and the one you'll need
for the lessons in this book, is worsted weight (sometimes
called 4-ply). It is readily available in a wide variety of
beautiful colours. Choose a light colour for practice—it
will be much easier to see the individual stitches.

Always read yarn labels carefully for information including
the following: how much yarn is in the skein, hank or ball,
in ounces or grams and in yards or metres; the type of
yarn; how to care for it; and sometimes how to pull the
yarn from the skein (and yes, there is a trick to this!). The
label usually bears a dye lot number, which assures you
that the colour of each skein with this same number is
identical. The same colour may vary from dye lot to dye
lot, creating unsightly variations in colour when a project
is finished—so when purchasing yarn for a project, be sure
to match the dye lot number on the skeins and purchase
enough to complete the project.

You'll need a blunt-pointed sewing needle, with an eye big
enough to carry the yarn, for weaving in ends and joining
pieces. You can use a size 16 steel tapestry needle, or
purchase a large plastic sewing needle called a yarn needle.

Crochet Hooks

Even though you're knitting, not crocheting, you'll need to
have a crochet hook handy for correcting mistakes, retrieving
dropped stitches and for some finishing techniques. (You
don't need to know how to crochet, though!)

The hook size you need depends on the thickness of the
yarn you are using for your project, and on the size of the
knitting needles.

Here's a handy chart to show you what size hook to use:

Knitting Needle Size	Crochet Hook Size
5, 6	F
7, 8, 9	G
10 and 10½	H
11 and 13	I
15 and 17	J

Knitting Needles

Knitting needles come in pairs of straight needles, each having a shaped point at one end and a knob at the other end so that the stitches won't slide off. Needles also come in sets of four double-pointed needles used for making small seamless projects, and in circular form with a point at each end.

You will most often use straight needles, which are readily available in many materials including aluminum, bamboo and plastic. The straight needles come in a variety of lengths, the most common being 10 inches and 14 inches. For our lessons, we will use the 10-inch length.

The needles also come in a variety of sizes, which refer to the diameter and thus the size of the stitch you can make with them. These are numbered from 0 (the smallest usually available) to 17 (the largest usually available). There are larger needles, but they are not used as often. For our lessons, we use a size 8 needle, an average size for use with worsted weight yarn.

Let's look at a knitting needle:

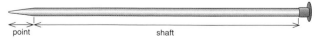

Now, with your yarn and needles ready, let's get started.

Lesson 1

Casting On

Knitting always starts with a row of foundation stitches worked onto one needle. Making a foundation row is called casting on. Although there are several ways of casting on, the following way is the easiest for beginners:

1. Make a slip knot on one needle as follows: Make a yarn loop, leaving about 4-inch length of yarn at free end.

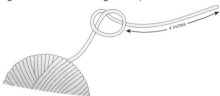

Insert knitting needle into loop and draw up yarn from free end to make a loop on needle.

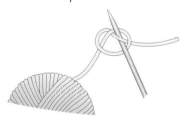

Pull yarn firmly, but not tightly, to form a slip knot on the shaft, not the point, of the needle. Pull yarn end to tighten the loop. This slip knot counts as your first stitch.

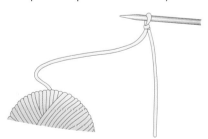

2. Place the needle with the knot in your left hand, placing the thumb and index finger close to the point of the needle, which helps you control it.

3. Hold the other needle with your right hand, again with your fingers close to the point. Grasp the needle firmly, but not tightly.

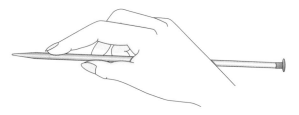

4. Your right hand controls the yarn coming from the ball. To help keep your tension even, hold the yarn loosely against the palm of your hand with three fingers, then up and over your index finger. These diagrams show how this looks from above the hand and beneath the hand.

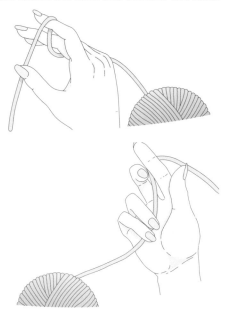

5. Insert the point of the right needle—from front to back—into the slip knot and under the left needle.

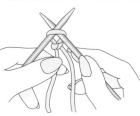

6. Continuing to hold left needle in your left hand, move left fingers over to brace right needle.

With right index finger, pick up the yarn from the ball,

and releasing right hand's grip on the right needle, bring yarn under and over the point of right needle.

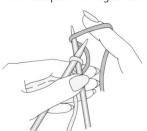

7. Returning right fingers to right needle, draw yarn through stitch with right needle.

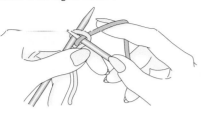

8. Slide left needle point into new stitch, then remove right needle.

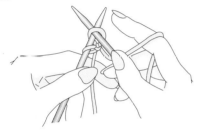

9. Pull ball of yarn gently, but not tightly, to make stitch snug on needle; you should be able to slip the stitch back and forth on the shaft of the needle easily.

You have now made one stitch, and there are two stitches on left needle (remember the slip knot counts as a stitch).

10. Insert point of right needle—from front to back—into stitch you've just made and under left needle.

Repeat Steps 6 through 10 for next stitch.

Continue repeating Steps 6 through 10 until you have 24 stitches on the left needle. Be sure to pull each stitch up, off the point and onto the shaft of the left needle.

Lesson 2

The Knit Stitch

All knitting is made up of only two basic stitches, the knit stitch and the purl stitch. These are combined in many ways to create different effects and textures. That means you're halfway to being a knitter, since you already learned the knit stitch as you practiced casting on! The first three steps of the knit stitch are exactly like casting on.

1. Hold the needle with the 24 cast-on stitches from Lesson 1 in your left hand. Insert the point of the right needle in the first stitch, from front to back, just as in casting on.

2. With right index finger, bring yarn from the skein under and over the point of the right needle.

3. Draw yarn through the stitch with the right needle point.

4. The next step now differs from casting on. Slip the loop on the left needle off, so the new stitch is entirely on the right needle.

Now you've completed your first knit stitch! Repeat these four steps in each stitch remaining on the left needle. When all stitches are on the right needle and the left needle is free, another row has been completed. Turn the right needle and place it in your left hand. Hold the free needle in your right hand. Work another row of stitches in same manner as last row, taking care not to work too tightly. Work 10 more rows of knit stitches.

The pattern formed by knitting every row is called *garter stitch* and looks the same on both sides. When counting rows in garter stitch, each raised ridge indicates you have knitted two rows.

Hint: When working on a garter stitch project it is helpful to place a small safety pin on the right side of the piece, as after a few rows both sides look the same.

Lesson 3

The Purl Stitch

The reverse of the knit stitch is called the purl stitch. Instead of inserting the right needle point from front to back under the left needle (as you did for the knit stitch), you will now insert it from back to front, in front of the left needle. Work as follows on the 24 stitches already on your needle.

1. Insert the right needle, from right to left, into the first stitch and in front of the left needle.

2. Holding the yarn in front of the work (side toward you), bring it around the right needle counterclockwise.

3. With the right needle, pull the yarn back through the stitch.

4. Slide the stitch off the left needle, leaving the new stitch on the right needle.

Your first purl stitch is now completed. Continue to repeat these three steps in every stitch across the row. The row you have just purled will be considered the wrong side of your work for the moment.

Now transfer the needle with the stitches from your right to left hand; the side of the work now facing you is called the right side of your work. Knit every stitch in the row; at end of row, transfer the needle with the stitches to your left hand, then purl every stitch in the row. Knit across another row, purl across another row.

Now stop and look at your work; by alternating knit and purl rows, you are creating one of the most frequently used stitch patterns in knitting, *stockinette stitch*.

Turn the work over to the right side; it should look like stitches in Photo A. The wrong side of the work should look like stitches in Photo B.

Continue with your practice piece, alternately knitting and purling rows, until you feel comfortable with the needles and yarn. As you work you'll see that your piece will begin to look more even.

Hint: Hold your work and hands in a comfortable relaxed position. The more comfortable and relaxed you are, the more even your work will be.

Lesson 4

Correcting Mistakes
Dropped Stitches

Each time you knit or purl a stitch, take care to pull the stitch off the left needle after completing the new stitch. Otherwise,

you will be adding stitches when you don't want to. If you let a stitch slip off the needle before you've knitted or purled it, it's called a dropped stitch. Even expert knitters drop a stitch now and then, but a dropped stitch must be picked up and put back on the needle. If not, the stitch will "run" down the length of the piece, just like a run in a stocking!

If you notice the dropped stitch right away, and it has not run down more than one row, you can usually place it back on the needle easily.

But, if it has dropped several rows, you'll find it easier to use a crochet hook to work the stitch back up to the needle.

On the knit side (right side of work) of the stockinette stitch, insert the crochet hook into the dropped stitch from front to back, under the horizontal strand in the row above.

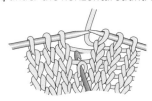

Hook the horizontal strand above and pull through the loop on the crochet hook. Continue in this manner until you reach the last row worked, then transfer the loop from the crochet hook to the left needle, being careful not to twist it.

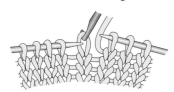

Unravelling Stitches

Sometimes it is necessary to unravel a large number of stitches, even down several rows, to correct a mistake. Whenever possible, carefully unravel the stitches one by one by putting the needle into the row below and undoing the stitch above, until the mistake is reached.

If several rows need to be unravelled, carefully slide all stitches off the needle and unravel each row down to the row in which the error occurred. Then unravel this row, stitch by stitch, placing each stitch, without twisting it, back on the needle in the correct position.

Lesson 5

Binding Off

Now you've learned how to cast on, knit and purl the stitches; next, you need to know how to take the stitches off the needle once you've finished a piece.

The process used to secure the stitches is called binding off. Let's bind off your practice piece; be careful to work loosely for this procedure, and begin with the right side (the knit side) of your work facing you.

Knit Bind-Off

1. Knit the first two stitches. Now insert the left needle into the first of the two stitches, the one you knitted first,

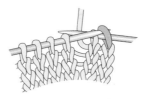

and pull it over the second stitch and completely off the needle. You have now bound off one stitch.

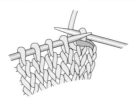

2. Knit one more stitch; insert the left needle into the first stitch on the right needle and pull the first stitch over the new stitch and completely off the needle. Another stitch is now bound off.

Repeat Step 2 four times more; now knit each of the remaining stitches on the left needle. You should have 18 stitches on the right needle, and you have bound off six stitches on the knit side of your work. *Note: The first of the 18 stitches was worked while binding off the last stitch at the beginning of the row.*

To bind off on the purl side, turn your practice piece so the wrong side of your work is facing you.

Purl Bind-Off

1. Purl the first two stitches. Now insert the left needle into the first stitch on the right needle,

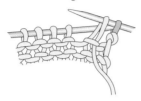

and pull it over the 2nd stitch and completely off the needle. You have now bound off one stitch.

2. Purl one more stitch; insert the left needle into the first stitch on the right needle and pull the first stitch over the new stitch and completely off the needle. Another stitch is bound off.

Repeat Step 2 four times more; now purl each of the 11 stitches remaining on the left needle for a total of 12 stitches on the right needle.

Turn your work so that the right side is facing you; bind off six stitches in the same manner that you bound off the first six stitches on this side, then knit remaining stitches.

Turn your work and bind off the remaining stitches on the wrong side; there will be one stitch left on the needle and you are ready to "finish off" or "end off" the yarn. To do this,

cut the yarn leaving about a 6-inch end. With the needle, draw this end up through the final stitch to secure it.

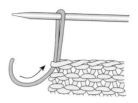

You have just learned to bind off knit stitches on the right side of your work and purl stitches on the wrong side of your work. When you wish to bind off in a pattern stitch, where some stitches in a row have been knitted and others purled, knit the knit stitches and purl the purl stitches as you work across the row.

Always bind-off loosely to maintain the same amount of stretch or "give" at the edge as in the rest of your work. If the bind off is too tight at the neckband ribbing of a pullover sweater, for example, the sweater will not fit over your head!

Hint: You can ensure the binding off being loose enough if you replace the needle in your right hand with a needle one size larger.

Lesson 6

Increasing

To shape knitted pieces, you will make them wider or narrower by increasing or decreasing a certain number of stitches from time to time.

Begin a new practice piece by casting on 12 stitches. Work four rows of garter stitch (remember this means you will knit every row); then on the next row, purl across (this purl side now becomes the wrong side of the work, since you will now begin working in stockinette stitch). Knit one more row, then purl one more row. You are now ready to practice increasing.

Although there are many ways to increase, this method is used most often.

Knit (or Purl) Two Stitches in One

1. On your practice piece (with the right side facing you), work as follows in the first stitch:

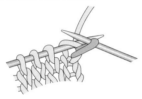

2. Insert the tip of the right needle from front to back into the stitch, and knit it in the usual manner but don't remove the stitch from the left needle.

Insert the needle (from front to back) into the back loop of the same stitch, and knit it again, this time slipping the stitch off the left needle. You have now increased one stitch.

Knit across the row until one stitch remains, then increase again by repeating Steps 1 and 2. You should now have 14 stitches.

Purl one row then knit one row, without increasing.

On your next row, the purl side, again increase in the first stitch. To increase on the purl side, insert the needle (from back to front) into the stitch; purl the stitch in the usual manner but don't remove it from the left needle. Then insert the needle (from back to front) into the back loop of the same stitch;

purl it again, this time slipping the stitch off. Then purl across to the last stitch; increase again. You should now have 16 stitches.

Now knit one row and purl one row without increasing.

Lesson 7

Decreasing
Method 1: Right Slanting Decrease
Knit (or Purl) Two Stitches Together
In this method, you simply knit two stitches as one. Knit the first stitch on your practice piece, then decrease as follows:

1. Insert the needle in usual manner but through the fronts of the next two stitches on the left needle.

2. Bring yarn under and over the point of the needle,

draw the yarn through both stitches,

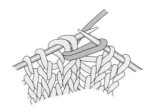

slip the stitches off the left needle and one new stitch will be on the right needle.

You have decreased one stitch. Knit across to the last three stitches; repeat Steps 1 and 2 again to decrease another stitch, then knit the last stitch. You should now have 14 stitches.

This decrease can also be worked on the purl side. On the next row of your practice piece, purl one stitch, then insert the needle in the fronts of next two stitches and purl them as if they were one stitch. Purl to the last three stitches, decrease again; purl remaining stitch.

Method 2: Left Slanting Decrease
Pass Slipped Stitch Over
This method is often used in the shaping of raglans or other pieces where a definite decrease line is desired. In the following samples the decrease is worked one stitch in from the edge. By working in one stitch from the edge, the decrease does not become a part of the seam.

To use this method you must first know how to "slip" a stitch. When instructions say to slip a stitch, this means you will slip it from the left needle to the right, without working it. To do this, insert right needle into the stitch as if you were going to purl it (even if it's a knit stitch); but instead of purling, slip the stitch from the left needle to the right needle.

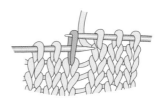

Note: Always insert the needle as to purl when slipping a stitch, unless instructions specify "slip as to knit"; in that case, insert the needle in the position for knitting, and slip the stitch in the same manner.

Now that you know how to slip a stitch, you can practice the second method of decreasing. On your practice piece, knit the first stitch. Instructions to decrease may read: "Slip 1, knit 1, pass slipped stitch over." To do this, work as follows:

1. Slip the next stitch, as to purl.

2. Knit the next stitch.

3. Pass the slipped stitch over the knitted stitch by using point of the left needle to lift the slipped stitch over the next stitch and completely off the needle.

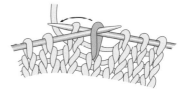

Knit to the last three stitches. Repeat Steps 1, 2 and 3. Then knit the last stitch.

This decrease can also be worked on the purl side. To do so, purl the first stitch. Slip next stitch, purl the next stitch, pass slipped stitch over purled stitch. Purl to the last three stitches, then repeat the purl decrease and purl the last stitch.

Hint: When slipping stitches the yarn is not moved unless specified in the instructions.

Decreasing, Alternate Method 2: Left Slanting Decrease
Slip, Slip, Knit
This decrease is similar in appearance to the previous method but has a smoother look because the stitch is not lifted or pulled up, which creates a slightly larger loop.

When this decrease is used the stitches are slipped as if to **knit** (see Note on page 17).

1. To practice this method, knit the first stitch, slip the next two stitches one at a time from the left to the right needle as if to knit.

2. Insert the left needle into the front of both stitches, bring the yarn around the needle as if knitting and lift the two stitches over and off the needle at the same time.

Knit to the last three stitches, repeat the slip, slip, knit the two slipped stitches together, then knit the last stitch. Purl one row.

Notice the two methods of decreasing. Method 1 causes the decreased stitch to slant from left to right, while in Method 2 the stitch slants from right to left. For a sweater, both methods are often used in the same row for a mirrored effect.

To practice this mirrored look, knit one stitch, decrease using either of the Method 2 decreases, knit to the last three stitches, knit two stitches together using Method 1 and knit the last stitch. Notice that both decreases slant towards the centre of your sample.

Lesson 8

Ribbing
Sometimes you want a piece of knitting to fit more closely—such as at the neck, wrists or bottom of a sweater. To do this, a combination of knit and purl stitches alternating in the same row, called ribbing, creates an elastic effect. To practice ribbing, start a new piece by casting on 24 stitches loosely. Always cast on loosely for ribbing, to provide enough stretch in the first row.

Knit Two, Purl Two Ribbing
Pattern Row: Knit two stitches, then bring yarn under the needle to the front of the work and purl two stitches; take the yarn under the needle to the back of the work and knit two stitches; yarn to front again, purl two stitches.

Note: You may tend to add stitches accidentally by forgetting to move the yarn to the front before purling, or to the back before knitting.

Remembering to move the yarn, repeat this knit two, purl two alternating pattern across the row.

Work this same Pattern Row 11 more times or until you feel comfortable with it. Your work should look like this:

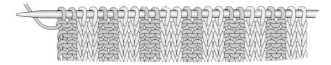

Hint: If you have trouble distinguishing a knit stitch or a purl stitch, remember that the smooth "v-shaped" stitches are knit stitches and the bumpy ones are purl stitches.

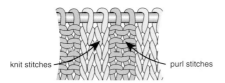

knit stitches — — purl stitches

Bind off loosely, remembering to knit the knit stitches and purl the purl stitches. Look at the work and see how the ribbing draws it in.

Knit One, Purl One Ribbing

This rib stitch pattern produces a finer ribbing, and is often used on baby clothes or on garments knitted with light weight yarns. Again cast on 24 stitches.

Pattern Row: Knit the first stitch, yarn under needle to front, purl the next stitch; yarn under needle to back, knit next stitch; yarn to front, purl next stitch. Continue across row, alternating one knit stitch with one purl stitch.

Work this same Pattern Row 11 more times or until you feel comfortable with this rib pattern. Your work should look like this:

Practice this ribbing for several more rows, then bind off in ribbing, knitting the knit (smooth) stitches and purling the purl (bumpy) stitches.

Lesson 9

Changing Yarn
Joining Yarn
New yarn should be added only at the beginning of a row, never in the middle of a row, unless this is required for a colour pattern change. To add yarn, tie the new strand around the old strand, making a knot at the edge of work, leaving at least a 4-inch end on both old and new strands. Then proceed to knit with the new yarn. The ends will be hidden later.

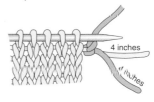

Carrying Yarn
When a yarn is repeated every several rows, it can be carried along the edge when not in use. At the beginning of the row, bring the carried colour under and over the colour just used and begin knitting (or purling).

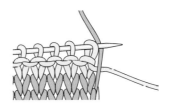

Lesson 10

Gauge & Measuring

This is the most important lesson of all, for if you don't work to gauge, your knitted garments will not fit as designed.

Gauge simply means the number of stitches per inch and the number of rows per inch, that result from a specified yarn worked with needles in a specified size. This was the information used by the designer when creating the project.

But, since everyone knits differently—some loosely, some tightly, some in between—the measurements of individual work will vary greatly, even when the knitters use exactly the same pattern and exactly the same size yarn and needles.

That's why you need to knit a gauge swatch before you actually start working on a project.

Needle sizes given in instructions are merely guides and should never be used without making a 4-inch square sample swatch to check your gauge. *It is your responsibility to make sure you achieve the gauge specified in the pattern.* To achieve this gauge, you may need to use a different needle size—either larger or smaller—than that specified in the pattern. Always change to larger or smaller needles if necessary to achieve gauge.

Here's how to check your gauge. At the beginning of every knit pattern you'll find a gauge given, like this (note the use of abbreviations):

Gauge

16 sts and 24 rows = 4 inches/10cm in stockinette st, with size 8 needles

This means that you will work your gauge swatch in stockinette stitch, and will try to achieve a gauge of 16 stitches and 24 rows to 4 inches. You must make a gauge swatch at least 4 inches square to adequately test your work.

Starting with the recommended size 8 needle, cast on 16 stitches. Work in stockinette stitch for 24 rows. Loosely bind off all stitches.

Place the swatch on a flat surface and pin it out, being careful not to stretch it. Measure the outside edges; the swatch should be 4 inches square.

Now measure the centre 2 inches from side to side, and count the actual stitches. There should be eight stitches in the 2 inches.

8 stitches = 2 inches

Then measure the centre 2 inches from top to bottom and count the rows per inch. There should be 12 rows in the 2 inches.

12 rows = 2 inches

If you have more stitches or rows per inch than specified, make another swatch with a size larger needles.

If you have fewer stitches or rows per inch than specified, make another swatch with a size smaller needles.

Making gauge swatches before beginning a garment takes time and is a bother. But if you don't make the effort to do this important step, you'll never be able to create attractive, well-fitting garments.

Once you've begun a garment, it's a good idea to keep checking your gauge every few inches; if you become relaxed, you may find yourself knitting more loosely; if you tense up, your knitting may become tighter. To keep your gauge, it may be necessary to change needle sizes in the middle of a garment.

For a swatch in garter stitch, every two rows form a ridge which needs to be taken into consideration when counting rows.

2 rows

Hint: Sometimes you'll find that you have the correct stitch gauge, but can't get the row gauge even with a change in needle size. If so, the stitch gauge is more important than the row gauge, with one exception: raglan sweaters. In knitting raglans, the armhole depth is based on row gauge, so you must achieve both stitch and row gauge.

Lesson 11

Reading Patterns

Knitting patterns are written in a special language, full of abbreviations, asterisks, parentheses, and other symbols and terms. These short forms are used so instructions will not take up too much space. They may seem confusing at first, but once understood, they are easy to follow.

Symbols

[ ] work instructions within brackets as many times as directed such as [k2, p2] twice.

* repeat instructions following the * as directed; thus, "rep from * twice" means after working the instructions once, repeat the instructions following the asterisk twice more (three times in all).

( ) parentheses are used to list the garment sizes and to provide additional information to clarify instructions.

Work in pattern as established is usually used when referring to a pattern stitch. The term means to continue following the pattern stitch as it is set up (established) on the needle. Work any subsequent increases or decreases in such a way that the established pattern remains the same (usually, working added stitches at the beginning or end of a row), outside the established pattern area.

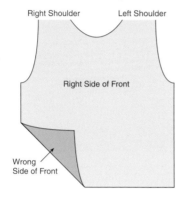

Work even means to continue to work in the pattern as established, without working any increases or decreases.

Following Size in Patterns

The patterns for garments include a variety of sizes. Each pattern is written for the smallest size pattern with changes in the number of stitches (or inches) for other sizes in parentheses. For example, the pattern will tell you how many stitches to cast on as follows:

Cast on 20 (23, 24) stitches.

You would cast on 20 stitches for the small size, 23 stitches for the medium size and 24 stitches for the large size. Depending on the pattern there may be more sizes or fewer sizes given. Check the measurements to determine the best size to make.

Before you begin knitting, it might be helpful to highlight or circle all the numbers for the size you are making throughout the pattern.

Lesson 12

Finishing

Many a well-knitted garment, worked exactly to gauge, ends up looking sloppy and amateurish, simply because of bad finishing. Finishing a knitted garment requires no special skill, but it does require time, attention and knowledge of basic techniques.

Picking Up Stitches

You will often need to pick up a certain number of stitches along an edge, such as around a sweater neckline or armhole, so that ribbing or an edging can be worked. The pattern instructions will usually clearly state where and how many stitches to pick up. Although this is not difficult, it is often done incorrectly, and the results look messy. Many times a circular needle is used for picking up stitches. For a neck edge, once the stitches are picked up, you begin knitting again in the first stitch and continue to work around the needle until the desired length is achieved.

To pick up a stitch, hold the knitting with the right side of the work facing you. Hold yarn from the skein behind the work, and hold a knitting needle in your right hand. Insert the point of the needle into the work from front to back, one stitch (at least two threads) from the edge; wrap the yarn around the needle as if knitting and draw the yarn through with the needle to the right side of the work making one stitch on the needle.

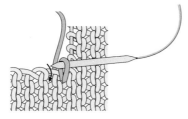

Pick up another stitch in the same manner, spacing stitches evenly along the edge.

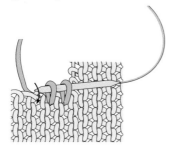

When picking up, pick up one stitch for each stitch when working across stitches in a horizontal row, and pick up about three stitches for every four rows when working along ends of rows. If a large number of stitches are to be picked up, it is best to mark off the edge into equal sections, then pick up the same number of stitches in each section.

For stitches that have been bound off along a neck edge, pick up through both loops of each stitch.

Sometimes stitches are placed on a holder when working the front and back of a garment. When picking up these stitches they can either be knit directly from the holder or slipped to another needle and knit from it, depending on how they were originally slipped onto the holder.

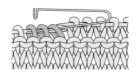

Blocking

Blocking simply means "setting" each piece into its final size and shape. (**Note:** *Be sure to check the yarn label before blocking, as some synthetic yarns and mohair yarns are ruined if they are blocked.*)

To block, moisten each piece first by dampening it with a light water spray. Then place each piece out on a padded flat surface (terry towelling provides adequate padding) right side up and away from direct sunlight. Referring to the small drawing or schematic in the pattern for the measurements for each piece, smooth out each piece to correct size and shape, using your fingers and the palms of your hands. Be sure to keep the stitches and rows in straight alignment. Use rust-proof straight pins to hold the edges in place. Let pieces dry completely before removing.

If further blocking is required, use steam from a steam iron. Hold the iron close to the knitted piece and allow the steam to penetrate the fabric. Never rest the iron directly on the piece—knitting should never have a pressed flat look. Let dry completely before removing.

Important Note: Never press ribbing, garter stitch, cables, or textured patterns as in Irish knits.

Sewing Seams

Your pattern will usually tell you in what order to assemble the pieces. Use the same yarn as used in the garment to sew the seams, unless the yarn is too thick, in which case, use a thinner yarn in a matching colour.

Invisible Seam

This seam gives a smooth and neat appearance, as it weaves the edges together invisibly from the right side.

To join horizontal edges, such as shoulder seams, sew the edges together as shown.

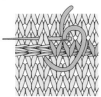

To join a front/back vertical edge to a horizontal sleeve edge, weave the edges together as shown.

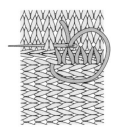

To join vertical edges, such as side seams or underarm sleeve seams, sew the edges together on the right side, pulling yarn gently until the edges meet.

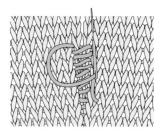

For pieces made using garter stitch, join vertical edges as shown.

Hint: *When seaming, do not draw the stitches too tight, as the joining should have the same stretch or give as in the knitted garment.*

Kitchener Stitch

This method of weaving with two needles is used for the toes of socks and flat seams. To weave the edges together and form an unbroken line of stockinette stitch, divide all stitches evenly onto two knitting needles—one behind the other. Thread yarn into tapestry needle. Hold needles with wrong sides together and work from right to left as follows:

Insert tapestry needle into first stitch on front needle as to purl. Draw yarn through stitch, leaving stitch on knitting needle.

Insert tapestry needle into the first stitch on the back needle as to purl. Draw yarn through stitch and slip stitch off knitting needle.

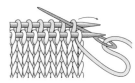

Insert tapestry needle into the next stitch on same (back) needle as to knit, leaving stitch on knitting needle.

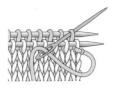

Insert tapestry needle into the first stitch on the front needle as to knit. Draw yarn through stitch and slip stitch off knitting needle.

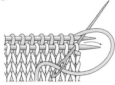

Insert tapestry needle into the next stitch on same (front) needle as to purl. Draw yarn through stitch, leaving stitch on knitting needle.

Repeat Steps 2 through 5 until one stitch is left on each needle. Then repeat Steps 2 and 4. Fasten off. Woven stitches should be the same size as adjacent knitted stitches.

Weaving in Ends

The final step is to weave in all the yarn ends securely. To do this, use a size 16 tapestry needle and weave the yarn end through the backs of stitches.

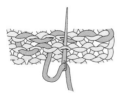

First weave the yarn about 2 inches in one direction and then 1 inch in the reverse direction. Cut off excess yarn.

If the ends are close to a seam weave the yarn back and forth along the edge of the seam.

Lesson 13

Substituting Yarn

When substituting a different yarn, you should stitch a swatch with the needle/hook size listed to make sure the yarn you have selected matches the gauge given in the pattern.

Changing Needle Size

If you need to stitch *more* stitches in your swatch to create the gauge listed, try the next size *smaller* needle/hook to see if this will give you the correct gauge.

If you need to stitch *fewer* stitches in your swatch to create the gauge listed, try the next size *larger* needle/hook to see if this will give you the gauge.

DETERMINE AMOUNT OF YARN NEEDED

General conversion amounts for yarns given generically. Yardages are approximations.

Lace (lace) weight:	1 ounce =	133 yards
Super fine (sock, fingering, baby) weight:	1 ounce =	170–175 yards
Fine (sport) weight:	1 ounce =	90–100 yards
Light (light worsted) weight:	1 ounce =	70–75 yards
Medium (worsted) weight:	1 ounce =	50 yards
Bulky (chunky) weight:	1 ounce =	30–35 yards
Super bulky (super chunky) weight:	1 ounce =	16–23 yards

Lesson 14

Special Techniques

Here are some intermediate techniques for increasing and binding off. Try these once you are proficient in the basic techniques.

Invisible Increase (M1)

There are several ways to make or increase one stitch.

Make 1 With Left Twist (M1L)

Insert left needle from front to back under the horizontal loop between the last stitch worked and next stitch on left needle.

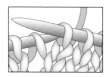

With right needle, knit into the back of this loop.

To make this increase on the purl side, insert left needle in same manner and purl into the back of the loop.

Make 1 With Right Twist (M1R)

Insert left needle from back to front under the horizontal loop between the last stitch worked and next stitch on left needle.

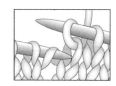

With right needle, knit into the front of this loop.

To make this increase on the purl side, insert left needle in same manner and purl into the front of the loop.

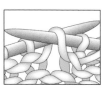

3-Needle Bind-Off

Use this technique for seaming two edges together, such as when joining a shoulder seam. Hold the edge stitches on two separate needles with right sides together.

With a third needle, knit together a stitch from the front needle with one from the back.

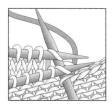

Repeat, knitting a stitch from the front needle with one from the back needle once more.

Slip the first stitch over the second.

Repeat knitting, a front and back pair of stitches together, then bind one off.

Standard Abbreviations

[ ] work instructions within brackets as many times as directed

( ) work instructions within parentheses in the place directed

** repeat instructions following the asterisks as directed

* repeat instructions following the single asterisk as directed

" inch(es)

beg begin/beginning
CC contrasting colour
ch chain stitch
cm centimetre(s)
cn cable needle
dec decrease/decreases/decreasing

dpn(s) double-pointed needle(s)
g gram
inc increase/increases/increasing
k knit
k2tog knit 2 stitches together
LH left hand
lp(s) loop(s)
m metre(s)
M1 make one stitch
MC main colour
mm millimetre(s)
oz ounce(s)
p purl
pat(s) pattern(s)
p2tog purl 2 stitches together
pm place marker

psso pass slipped stitch over
p2sso pass 2 slipped stitches over
rem remain/remaining
rep repeat(s)
rev St st reverse stockinette stitch
RH right hand
rnd(s) round(s)
RS right side
skp slip, knit, pass stitch over—one stitch decreased
sk2p slip 1, knit 2 together, pass slip stitch over the knit 2 together—2 stitches have been decreased
sl slip

sl 1k slip 1 knitwise
sl 1p slip 1 purlwise
sl st slip stitch(es)
ssk slip, slip, knit these 2 stitches together—a decrease
st(s) stitch(es)
St st stockinette stitch/stocking stitch
tbl through back loop(s)
tog together
WS wrong side
wyib with yarn in back
wyif with yarn in front
yd(s) yard(s)
yfwd yarn forward
yo yarn over

Standard Yarn Weight System
Categories of yarn, gauge ranges, and recommended needle sizes

Yarn Weight Symbol & Category Names	① SUPER FINE	② FINE	③ LIGHT	④ MEDIUM	⑤ BULKY	⑥ SUPER BULKY
Type of Yarns in Category	Sock, Fingering, Baby	Sport, Baby	DK, Light Worsted	Worsted, Afghan, Aran	Chunky, Craft, Rug	Bulky, Roving
Knit Gauge* Ranges in Stockinette Stitch to 4 inches	21–32 sts	23–26 sts	21–24 sts	16–20 sts	12–15 sts	6–11 sts
Recommended Needle in Metric Size Range	2.25–3.25mm	3.25–3.75mm	3.75–4.5mm	4.5–5.5mm	5.5–8mm	8mm
Recommended Needle Canada/U.S. Size Range	1 to 3	3 to 5	5 to 7	7 to 9	9 to 11	11 and larger

* GUIDELINES ONLY: The above reflect the most commonly used gauges and needle sizes for specific yarn categories.

KNITTING IN THE ROUND WITH CIRCULAR NEEDLES

Getting Started

New Term & Abbreviation
working end: the end of the yarn that is attached to the ball

You've been knitting things back and forth on straight needles, turning at the end of every row. How would you like to just knit, round after round, without turning at all, and then have no seams to sew up when you are finished knitting?

You can! A method called circular knitting makes tubes of knitted fabric in any size. You can make hats, socks, mittens and sweaters this way.

To knit on circular needles:

Instructions

Cast on the desired number of stitches onto the needle just as you would onto straight needles. Start practicing with a 16-inch circular needle. You need to have enough stitches to fill the needle.

Spread the stitches evenly across the needle and make sure they are not twisted (Photo 1).

Photo 1

Hold the needles so the working end of yarn is on the right-hand tip of the needle, and the first stitch you cast on is on the left-hand tip of the needle (Photo 2).

Photo 2

Place a stitch marker on the right-hand needle. The marker is between the first and last stitch you cast on and marks the beginning of a round. Stitch markers can be a loop of yarn in a contrasting colour or a purchased plastic stitch marker (Photo 3).

Photo 3

Using the working end, knit the first stitch on the left-hand needle. This is the first stitch you cast on (Photo 4).

Photo 4

In patterns, the previous steps are usually called "join, being careful not to twist."

Keep knitting all the stitches, sliding them along the needle as you work them from the left tip to the right tip.

When you reach the stitch marker, slip it to the right-hand needle, then keep knitting.

Keep knitting round and round until your tube is as long as you need (Photo 5).

Photo 5

KNITTING IN THE ROUND WITH DOUBLE-POINTED NEEDLES

New Term & Abbreviation
dpn(s): double-pointed needle(s)

Sometimes you want to knit a seamless tube that is narrower than you can fit on a circular needle. That's when you need double-pointed needles. Sleeves, socks and mittens may be knit in the round on double-pointed needles.

Double-pointed needles are short needles with points on both ends. They are used in sets of four or five.

Instructions

To knit on four double-pointed needles:

Cast all the stitches onto one needle.

Slide one third of the stitches onto each of two other needles (Photo 1).

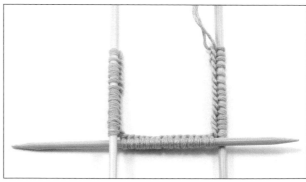

Photo 1

Make sure the stitches are straight across all the needles; then fold the two end needles around so the last stitch cast on and the first stitch cast on are next to each other, with the working end on the right (Photo 2).

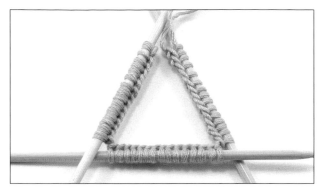

Photo 2

Insert the tip of the fourth needle into the first stitch you cast on (Photo 3). Use the working end of yarn to knit all the stitches across this needle (Photo 4).

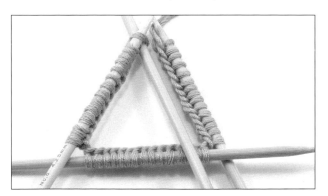

Photo 3

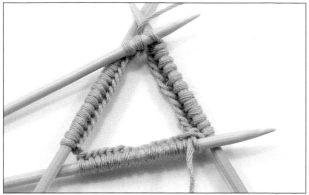

Photo 4

Now use the needle that just became free to knit all the stitches off the next needle.

Step 6: Keep knitting around, using the free needle to knit stitches off the next needle in line (Photo 5).

Photo 5

Although it looks tricky because there are so many needles, it's not hard at all. You are only knitting from one needle to another just as you have been doing all along!

RIDGED MOBIUS

This one-size-fits-all shoulder warmer will go on the town or keep you cozy while relaxing at home.

Design by Zena Low

Skill Level

EASY

Size
Approx 40 x 14 inches

Materials
Bulky weight yarn (86 yds/80g per ball):
   2 balls water
Size 15 (10mm) 36-inch circular needle or size
   needed to obtain gauge
Stitch marker

Gauge
10 sts and 12 rows = 4 inches/10cm in St st
To save time, take time to check gauge.

Pattern Note
Usually when joining to work in the round, you would take care not to twist the stitches. With this project, you must insert a twist to achieve the shape.

Mobius
Cast on 90 sts. Join and work in rnds, making sure there is 1 twist in the sts, marking beg of rnd.

Rnds 1–8: Knit.

Rnds 9–16: Purl.

Rnds 17–22: Knit.

Rnds 23–27: Purl.

Rnds 28–32: Knit.

Rnds 33–40: Purl.

Bind off all sts purlwise. ■

Ridged Mobius

Sample project was knit with Solo (72 per cent acrylic/28 per cent polyester) from Bernat.

TOASTY FRIEND

Choose this soft layer for keeping shoulders warm and cozy. It's a great choice for any age!

Design by Cecily Glowik

Skill Level

EASY

Sizes

Woman's small (medium, large, extra-large, 2X-large) Instructions are given for smallest size, with larger sizes in parentheses. When only 1 number is given, it applies to all sizes.

Finished Measurements

Bottom circumference: 48 (51½, 54¾, 58¼, 61¾) inches
Length to collar: 13½ (13½, 14½, 14½, 14½) inches

Materials

Bulky weight yarn (110 yds/100g per skein):
  5 (5, 6, 6, 7) skeins light brown
Size 10½ (6.5mm) 16-, 29- and 36-inch circular needles or size needed to obtain gauge
Size 11 (8mm) 16-inch circular needle (optional)
Stitch markers, 1 in CC for beg of rnd
Tapestry needle

Gauge

14 sts and 20 rows = 4 inches/10cm in St st
To save time, take time to check gauge.

Special Abbreviation

Inc1 (lifted increase): Inc 1 st as follows: before marker–k1 in row below next st, k1; following marker– k1, k1 2 rows below last st worked.

Pattern Stitch

Lace (multiple of 12 sts)

Rnd 1: *P3, yo, k4, k2tog, k3, rep from * around.

Rnd 2: *P3, k1, yo, k4, k2tog, k2, rep from * around.

Rnd 3: *P3, k2, yo, k4, k2tog, k1, rep from * around.

Rnd 4: *P3, k3, yo, k4, k2tog, rep from * around.

Rep Rnds 1–4 for pat.

Pattern Notes

Wrap begins with long collar, followed by a raglan-shaped body.

Change to longer needle when stitches no longer fit comfortably on needle in use.

A chart for the Lace pattern is included for those preferring to work from charts.

(Optional) Cast on and bind off with a needle 1 size larger than project needle to ensure loose edges.

Toasty Friend
Sample project was knit with
Baby Alpaca Grande (100 per
cent baby alpaca) from Plymouth
Yarn Co.

Wrap
Collar

With 16-inch needle, loosely cast on 64 (64, 72, 72, 80) sts, place marker for beg of rnd and join, being careful not to twist sts.

Work even in k4, p4 rib for 11 inches.

Body

Next rnd: *K4, M1, p4, M1; rep from * around. (80, 80, 90, 90, 100 sts)

Work 4 rnds in k4, p6 rib.

Work 4 rnds in St st.

Next rnd: *K30 (30, 33, 33, 36), place marker, k10 (10, 12, 12, 14), place marker; rep from * once to end of rnd marker.

Inc rnd: *Inc1, knit to marker, Inc1, sl marker; rep from * around. (88, 88, 98, 98, 108 sts)

Rep Inc rnd [every other rnd] 2 (4, 4, 5, 5) times, then [every 4th rnd] 8 times. (168, 184, 194, 202, 212 sts)

Work even in St st until piece measures approx 8½ (8½, 9½, 9½, 9½) inches from end of rib or 5 inches less than desired length.

Next rnd: Knit, and inc 0 (dec 4, dec 2, inc 2, inc 4) sts evenly around. (168, 180, 192, 204, 216 sts)

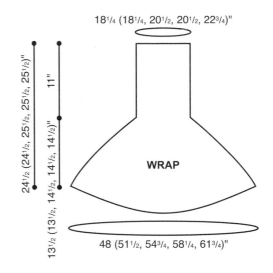

18¼ (18¼, 20½, 20½, 22¾)"

24½ (24½, 25½, 25½, 25½)"

11"

13½ (13½, 14½, 14½, 14½)"

WRAP

48 (51½, 54¾, 58¼, 61¾)"

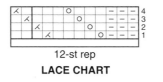

12-st rep

LACE CHART

STITCH KEY
- ⊟ Purl
- ⊙ Yarn over
- ☐ Knit
- ⊠ K2tog

[Rep Rnds 1–4 of Lace pat] 5 times, then work Rnds 1–3.

Bind off very loosely in pat using larger needle if necessary.

Finishing

Weave in ends. Block piece to finished measurements. ∎

ICY BLUE SHELL

The interesting Dragon Skin front panel only looks hard to make!

Design by Kennita Tully

Skill Level

EASY

Sizes

Woman's small (medium, large, extra-large, 2X-large) Instructions are given for smallest size, with larger sizes in parentheses. When only 1 number is given, it applies to all sizes.

Finished Measurements

Chest: 34 (38, 42, 46, 50) inches
Length: 17 (18, 19, 20, 22) inches

Materials

Worsted weight yarn (76 yds/50g per ball):
   5 (6, 7, 8, 10) balls robin's egg blue
Size 10½ (6.5mm) 16- and 32-inch circular
   needles or size needed to obtain gauge
Stitch markers
Stitch holders

4 MEDIUM

Gauge

16 sts and 20 rows = 4 inches/10cm in St st
17½ sts and 20 rows = 4 inches/10cm in Dragon Skin pat
To save time, take time to check gauge.

Special Abbreviation

M1 (Make 1): Inc by k1 in back of strand between st just worked and next st on LH needle.

Pattern Stitches

Dragon Skin Side Panel (panel of 11 sts)

Rnd 1 and all odd-numbered rnds: Knit.

Rnd 2: M1, ssk, k4, k2tog, k3, M1.

Rnd 4: M1, k1, ssk, k2, k2tog, k4, M1.

Rnd 6: M1, k2, ssk, k2tog, k5, M1.

Rnd 8: M1, k3, ssk, k4, k2tog, M1.

Rnd 10: M1, k4, ssk, k2, k2tog, k1, M1.

Rnd 12: M1, k5, ssk, k2tog, k2, M1. Rep Rnds 1–12 for pat.

Dragon Skin Centre Panel (panel of 24 sts)

Rnd 1 and all odd-numbered rnds: Knit.

Rnd 2: M1, ssk, k4, k2tog, k3, M1, k2, M1, k3, ssk, k4, k2tog, M1.

Rnd 4: M1, k1, ssk, k2, k2tog, k4, M1, k2, M1, k4, ssk, k2, k2tog, k1, M1.

Rnd 6: M1, k2, ssk, k2tog, k5, M1, k2, M1, k5, ssk, k2tog, k2, M1.

Rnd 8: M1, k3, ssk, k4, k2tog, M1, k2, M1, ssk, k4, k2tog, k3, M1.

Rnd 10: M1, k4, ssk, k2, k2tog, k1, M1, k2, M1, k1, ssk, k2, k2tog, k4, M1.

Rnd 12: M1, k5, ssk, k2tog, [k2, M1] twice, k2, ssk, k2tog, k5, M1.

Rep Rnds 1–12 for pat.

Pattern Note
Work all decreases 1 stitch in from edge.

Body
Cast on 138 (154, 170, 186, 202) sts, place marker and join without twisting.

Knit across 56 (64, 72, 80, 88) sts, place marker (back), work Dragon Skin Side Panel over 11 left-side sts, place marker, knit across 18 (22, 26, 30, 34) sts, place marker, work Dragon Skin Centre Panel over 24 sts, place marker, knit across 18 (22, 26, 30, 34) sts, place marker, work Dragon Skin Side Panel over 11 right-side sts.

Shape sides
Continue to work in established pats, and *at the same time*, on Rnds 6, 18 and 24, at beg of rnd ssk, work to 2 sts before next marker, k2tog, work side panel, ssk, work to 2 sts before side panel, k2tog. Work even in pat until completion of Rnd 35. (126, 142, 158, 174, 190 sts)

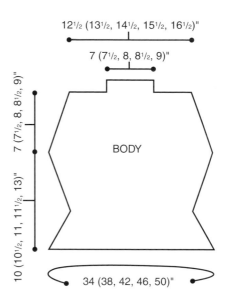

12½ (13½, 14½, 15½, 16½)"

7 (7½, 8, 8½, 9)"

7 (7½, 8, 8½, 9)"

10 (10½, 11, 11½, 13)"

BODY

34 (38, 42, 46, 50)"

On Rnds 36, 48 and 60, at beg of rnd, M1, work to next marker, M1, work side panel, M1, work to next side panel, M1. (138, 154, 170, 186, 202 sts)

Work even until body measures approx 10 (10½, 11, 11½, 13) inches, ending with an odd-numbered rnd.

Divide for front & back
Knit across back sts, knit 5 sts of left side panel, turn. Purl across back sts and 5 sts of right side panel. Leave front sts on holder or spare needle.

Shape back armholes
Working back and forth in St st over these 66 (74, 82, 90, 98) sts, dec 1 st at each side [every other row] 8 (10, 12, 14, 16) times. (50, 54, 58, 62, 66 sts)

Work even until armhole measures approx 7 (7½, 8, 8½, 9) inches, place rem sts on holder.

Front

Maintaining centre pat, work on rem 72 (80, 88, 96, 104) front sts, dec 1 st at each edge [every other row] 8 (10, 12, 14, 16) times as for back until front measures same as back. (56, 60, 64, 68, 72 sts)

Join shoulders

Sl back shoulders on needle. Join first and last 11 (12, 13, 14, 15) sts for shoulders, using 3-Needle Bind-Off (see page 26).

Neck Band

With 16-inch circular needle, knit across rem 34 (36, 38, 40, 42) front sts and 28 (30, 32, 34, 36) back sts from back and join, working a total of 4 rnds and continuing Dragon Skin Centre Panel into band. Bind off all sts. ■

Icy Blue Shell
Sample project was knit with Italian Ice (61 per cent cotton/ 26 per cent linen/13 per cent viscose) from Knit One, Crochet Too.

DOT & DASH PULLOVER

Two yarns combine for spectacular results. The long-repeat variegated main colour is interspersed with contrast yarn for a lovely effect.

Design by Lois S. Young

Skill Level

INTERMEDIATE

Sizes
Woman's small (medium, large, extra-large) Instructions are given for smallest size, with larger sizes in parentheses. When only 1 number is given, it applies to all sizes.

Finished Measurements
Chest: 36 (40, 44, 48) inches
Length: 22 (23½, 25, 26½) inches

Materials
Worsted weight yarn (100 yds/50g per ball):
  8 (10, 12, 14) balls rose quartz (MC)
Lace weight yarn (225 yds/25g per ball):
  2 (3, 3, 4) balls soft seafoam (CC)
Size 5 (3.5 mm) 16- and 29-inch circular
  needles and double-pointed needles
Size 7 (4.5mm) 16- and 29-inch circular needles and
  double-pointed needles or size needed to obtain gauge
Stitch markers, including 1 which can be moved from
  rnd to rnd
Stitch holders

Gauge
20 sts and 22 rows = 4 inches/10cm in pat
To save time, take time to check gauge.

Special Abbreviations
Sssk: Sl 3 sts individually as if to purl, return them to LH needle in this position, k3tog-tbl.

CDD (Central Double Decrease): Sl next 2 sts as if to k2tog, k1, p2sso.

Pattern Stitches
Seed St (even number of sts, worked in rnds)

Rnd 1: *K1, p1; rep from * around.

Rnd 2: *P1, k1; rep from * around.

Rep Rnds 1 and 2 for pat.

Dots & Dashes (worked in rnds)

Rnds 1 and 2: With MC, knit around.

Rnd 3: *K1 MC, k1 CC, k2 MC, k3 CC, k1 MC; rep from * around.

Rnd 4: *K1 MC, p1 CC, k2 MC, p3 CC, k1 MC; rep from * around.

Rnds 5–8: With MC, knit around.

Rnd 9: *K3 CC, k2 MC, k1 CC, k2 MC; rep from * around.

Dot & Dash Pullover
Sample project was knit with
Paint Box (100 per cent wool)
and Douceur et Soie (65 per cent
baby mohair/35 per cent silk)
from Knit One, Crochet Too.

Rnd 10: *P3 CC, k2 MC, p1 CC, k2 MC; rep from * around.

Rnds 11 and 12: With MC, knit around.

Rep Rnds 1–12 for pat.

Dots & Dashes (worked in rows)

Row 1 (RS): With MC, knit across.

Row 2: With MC, purl across.

Row 3: *K1 MC, k1 CC, k2 MC, k3 CC, k1 MC; rep from * across.

Row 4: *P1 MC, k1 CC, p2 MC, k3 CC, p1 MC; rep from * across.

Rows 5–8: [Rep Rows 1 and 2] twice.

Row 9: *K3 CC, k2 MC, k1 CC, k2 MC; rep from * across.

Row 10: *K3 CC, p2 MC, k1 CC, p2 MC; rep from * across.

Rows 11 and 12: Rep Rows 1 and 2.

Pattern Notes
Use 2 strands of contrasting colour yarn held together.

Sweater is worked in 1 piece. Body and sleeves are worked circularly to the underarms, then joined for yoke. Yoke is worked back and forth.

To make sleeves match, begin each sleeve at the same point of main colour repeat.

Underarm stitches are placed on holders and later woven together using Kitchener Stitch (see page 24). These stitches could also be bound off and sewn together.

Change from double-pointed needles to shorter circular needles when there are sufficient sleeve stitches.

Body
With smaller 29-inch circular needle, cast on 152 (172, 192, 212) sts. Join without twisting, place beg of rnd marker. Work 6 rnds Seed St, inc 16 (12, 16, 12) sts evenly on last rnd. (168, 184, 208, 224 sts)

Change to larger 29-inch needle and work even in pat until body measures 13½ (14½, 15½, 16½) inches, ending with an even-numbered rnd.

Divide for yoke
Work 36 (39, 44, 47) sts for left front, work and place on holder 1 st for centre neck, work 36 (39, 44, 47) sts for right front, work and place on holder 12 (14, 16, 18) sts for underarm, work 71 (77, 87, 93) sts for back, work and place on holder 12 (14, 16, 18) sts for underarm. Cut yarn and set aside.

Sleeves
With smaller dpns, cast on 40 (44, 48, 52) sts divided on 3 needles. Join without twisting, place beg of rnd marker. Work 8 rnds Seed St, inc 0 (4, 0, 4) sts evenly on last rnd. (40, 48, 48, 56 sts)

Change to larger dpns and work pat in rnds. Always beg and end each rnd with k1 in MC. Inc 1 st [every 5th rnd] 14 (14, 18, 18) times, working added sts into pat. (68, 76, 84, 92 sts)

Work even until sleeve measures 17½ (18½, 19½, 20) inches, ending on same pat rnd as body. Work and place on holder 6 (7, 8, 9) sts for first half of underarm, work and place on separate holder 56 (62, 68, 74) sts for raglan sleeve, work and place on holder 6 (7, 8, 9) sts for 2nd half of underarm, cut yarn, set aside.

Rep for 2nd sleeve.

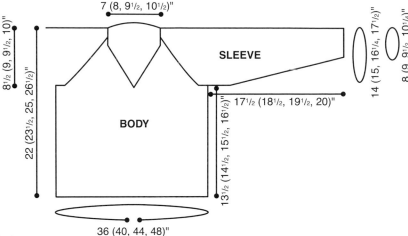

Yoke

Beg at centre front, leaving centre front st on holder. With RS facing, work 36 (39, 44, 47) right front sts, place raglan marker, remove from holder and work 56 (62, 68, 74) sleeve sts, place raglan marker, work 71 (77, 87, 93) back sts, place raglan marker, remove from holder and work 56 (62, 68, 74) sleeve sts, place raglan marker, work 36 (39, 44, 47) left front sts. (255, 277, 311, 335 sts)

Beg working back and forth in rows, continuing to work the pat stitch. Keep first and last sts of each rnd and 1 st before and 1 st after each raglan marker in St st in MC. Dec 1 st at beg and end of row and each side of raglan markers [every RS row] 12 (14, 14, 15) times. Dec 1 st at beg and end of row [every 4th row] 4 (5, 5, 6) times, and *at the same time*, continue to dec 1 st each side of raglan markers every RS row.

For last row with front dec, work sssk at beg of row and k3tog at end to dec front sts into sleeve. Continue to dec

1 st on each side of sleeve and on back [every RS row] 4 (5, 6, 6) times, ending with a WS row. Cut yarn. (8, 8, 8, 12 sts in each sleeve and 23, 27, 27, 28 sts on back neck)

Neck Band

With smaller 16-inch circular needle, remove from holder and knit centre front st, pick up and knit 47 (51, 55, 58) sts evenly along right front yoke, work 39 (43, 43, 52) sts of sleeve tops and back neck, pick up and knit 47 (51, 55, 58) sts evenly along left front yoke, place removable end of rnd marker on centre st. Join and work 6 rnds Seed St, working CDD over 3 centre front sts every rnd. Bind off in pat.

Assembly

Weave underarm seams using Kitchener Stitch (see page 24).

Block. ■

YUKON PULLOVER

With big needles and chunky yarn, you will have a sporty pullover to wear in no time.

Design by Kennita Tully

Skill Level

EASY

Sizes

Adult's small (medium, large, extra-large) Instructions are given for smallest size, with larger sizes in parentheses. When only 1 number is given, it applies to all sizes.

Finished Measurements

Chest: 37¾ (41½, 45, 49) inches
Length: 23 (24, 25, 26) inches

Materials

Bulky weight yarn (60 yds/100g per ball):
 8 (9, 10, 11) balls purple multicolour
Size 15 (10mm) double-pointed needles, 16- and 29-inch
 circular needles or size needed to obtain gauge
Stitch markers
Stitch holders

Gauge

8½ sts and 12 rnds = 4 inches/10cm in St st
To save time, take time to check gauge.

Body

With longer circular needle, cast on 40 (44, 48, 52) sts, place marker, cast on 40 (44, 48, 52) more sts. (80, 88, 96, 104 sts)

Join without twisting, place marker between first and last st.

Work in k1, p1 rib for 4 rnds.

Change to St st and work even until body measures 13 (13½, 14, 14½) inches.

Removing markers, place 6 (6, 8, 8) sts at each underarm on separate holders, and 34 (38, 40, 44) sts on each of 2 more separate holders for front and back.

Sleeves

With dpns, cast on 18 (20, 20, 20) sts. Join without twisting, place marker between first and last st.

Work in k1, p1 rib for 4 rnds, change to St st.

Changing to circular needle when needed, [inc 1 st each side of marker every 6th (5th, 4th, 4th) rnd] 7 (4, 1, 6) times, then every 0 (6th, 5th, 5th) rnd 0 (4, 8, 4) times. (32, 36, 38, 40 sts)

Work even until sleeve measures 16¾ (17½, 17½, 18) inches, ending last rnd 3 (3, 4, 4) sts before marker. Removing marker, place next 6 (6, 8, 8) sts on holder for underarm. Place rem sts on 2nd holder.

Yukon Pullover
Sample project was knit with Yukon Print (35 per cent mohair/35 per cent wool/30 per cent acrylic) from Plymouth Yarn Co.

Join sleeves & body

Place marker between each section, knit 34 (38, 40, 44) sts for front, 26 (30, 30, 32) sts for right sleeve, 34 (38, 40, 44) sts for back, 26 (30, 30, 32) sts for left sleeve. Place marker to mark end of rnd. (120, 136, 140, 152 sts)

Mark this last rnd at centre front. Work even for 1½ inches above marker.

Begin raglan yoke shaping

Dec rnd: [K2, k2tog, k to marker, ssk, k2] 4 times.

[Rep dec rnd every 2nd (3rd, 3rd, 3rd) rnd] 10 (1, 4, 1) times, then every 0 (2nd, 2nd, 2nd) rnd 0 (11, 8, 12) times.

At the same time, when yoke measures 5½ (6, 6½, 7) inches above centre front marker, beg front neck shaping.

Neck shaping

Work to centre 6 (6, 8, 8) sts, place centre 6 (6, 8, 8) sts on hold, turn.

Working in rows from this point, [dec 1 st at each side of neck every other row] 3 times.

Work until raglan dec are complete. (32, 32, 36, 40 sts)

Piece should measure approx 23 (24, 25, 26) inches. Leave rem sts on needle and cut yarn.

Collar

With 16-inch circular needle and RS facing, pick up and knit 5 (6, 6, 6) sts along left neck edge, knit 6 (6, 8, 8) sts from front neck holder, pick up and knit 5 (6, 6, 6) sts along right neck edge, knit rem sts from needle. (48, 50, 56, 60 sts)

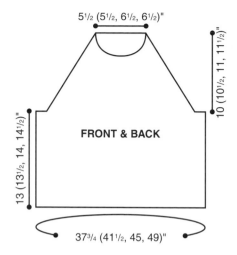

5½ (5½, 6½, 6½)"

10 (10½, 11, 11½)"

FRONT & BACK

13 (13½, 14, 14½)"

37¾ (41½, 45, 49)"

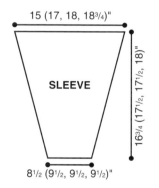

15 (17, 18, 18¾)"

16¾ (17½, 17½, 18)"

SLEEVE

8½ (9½, 9½, 9½)"

Join, place marker between first and last st.

Work even in St st for 2 (2, 3, 3) inches, then work 4 rnds in k1, p1 rib.

Bind off in ribbing.

Finishing

Sew underarm sleeve sts to underarm body sts, using Kitchener Stitch (see page 24). ■

CHIC & CABLED TOP

This is the perfect cabled pullover for first-time "cablers." These wavelike cables will create a sweater that is just right for the beach.

Design by Kathy Sasser

Skill Level

INTERMEDIATE

Sizes
Woman's small (medium, large, extra-large, 2X-large)
Instructions are given for smallest size, with larger sizes in parentheses. When only 1 number is given, it applies to all sizes.

Finished Measurements
Chest: 36 (40, 44, 48, 52) inches
Length: 22 (22½, 23, 23½, 24) inches

Materials
Worsted weight yarn (249 yds/125g per skein):
   4 (5, 6, 7, 7) skeins green
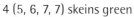
Size 6 (4mm) 24-inch circular needle
Size 7 (4.5mm) 24-inch circular needle or size needed to obtain gauge
Stitch markers
Cable needle
Safety pins
Stitch holders
Tapestry needle

Gauge
20 sts and 26 rows = 4 inches/10cm in St st on larger needle

To save time, take time to check gauge.

Special Abbreviations
C6B (Cable 6 Back): Sl next 3 sts to cn and hold in back; k3, then k3 from cn.

C6F (Cable 6 Front): Sl next 3 sts to cn and hold in front; k3, then k3 from cn.

Pattern Stitch
Wavy Cable (6-st panel)

Rnds 1–7: K6.

Rnd 8: C6B.

Rnds 9–15: K6.

Rnd 16: C6F.

Rep Rnds 1–16 for pat.

Pattern Notes
Sweater is worked in the round to armholes, then divided and worked back and forth; the sleeves are worked back and forth.

When working in rows, keep cable panel in established pat by knitting the knit sts and purling the purl sts as they face you on both sides and working cables on correct RS rows.

Body
With smaller needle, cast on 180 (200, 220, 240, 260) sts; place marker for beg of rnd and join, being careful not to twist sts.

Set-up rnd: K90 (100, 110, 120, 130) for front, place marker for right side seam line, k90 (100, 110, 120, 130) sts for back.

Knit 5 rnds, marking last rnd with a safety pin at centre front.

Next rnd: Change to larger needle and knit.

Next rnd (Cable 1 setup): K6 (7, 9, 11, 13), place marker, inc 3 sts evenly across next 18 sts to form 21-st cable panel, place marker, knit to end of rnd. (183, 203, 223, 243, 263 sts)

Rnds 1–32: Knit to first marker, sl marker, p3, work Wavy Cable pat, p3, k9, sl marker, knit to end of rnd.

Next rnd (Cable 2 setup): Knit to first marker, sl marker, *p3, work Wavy Cable pat; rep from * once, p3, sl marker, knit to end of rnd.

Continue in pats as established until piece measures 13½ (14, 14, 14, 14½) inches from safety pin, ending on any odd-numbered rnd.

Left Front & Neck Shaping
Next row (RS): Work 40 (44, 48, 53, 57) sts in pat, sl rem sts to smaller circular needle for holder; turn.

Dec row (WS): P1, p2tog, work to end of row. (39, 43, 47, 52, 56 sts)

Continue in pats as established and rep Dec row [every other row] 7 (8, 9, 9, 10) times. (32, 35, 38, 43, 46 sts)

Work even until left front measures 8½ (8½, 9, 9½, 9½) inches from beg of armhole, ending with a RS row.

Next row (WS): Removing markers, purl to 1 st before marker, [k2tog, k1, p6] 3 times, purl to end of row. (29, 32, 35, 40, 43 sts)

Place sts on a holder.

Right Front
Place 16 (18, 20, 20, 22) centre front sts on a st holder.

Attach yarn to next st on LH needle and with larger needle, knit to side marker, turn. (37, 41, 45, 50, 54 sts)

Dec row (WS): Purl to last 3 sts, ssp, p1. (36, 40, 44, 49, 53 sts)

Continue in St st and rep Dec row [every other row] 7 (8, 9, 9, 10) times. (29, 32, 35, 40, 43 sts)

Work even until right front measures same as left front to shoulder.

Place sts on a holder.

Back
With RS facing, attach yarn to back at right side edge.

With larger needle, work in St st until back measures same as front to shoulder.

Place sts on holder or spare needle.

Chic & Cabled Top
Sample project was knit with
Super 10 Worsted (100 per cent
cotton) from S.R. Kertzer

Left Sleeve

**With smaller needle, cast on 44 (48, 48, 50, 52) sts; do not join.

Beg with a RS row, work in St st for 6 rows.

Place a safety pin at beg and end of last row.

Change to larger needle.**

Inc 1 st each end [every 4 (5, 4, 4, 4) rows] 8 (18, 6, 12, 3) times, then [every 5 (6, 5, 5, 5) rows] 14 (2, 16, 12, 20) times. (88, 88, 92, 98, 98 sts)

Work even until sleeve measures 16½ (16½, 17, 17½, 18) inches from safety pins.

Bind off.

Right Sleeve

Work as for left sleeve from ** to **.

Work inc as for left sleeve and *at the same time* work centre cable panel as follows:

Set-up row (RS): K17 (19, 19, 20, 21), place marker, inc 2 sts evenly across next 10 sts to form 12-st cable panel, place marker, k17 (19, 19, 20, 21) sts. (46, 50, 50, 52, 54 sts)

Rows 1, 3, 5, 7 (WS): Purl to marker, sl marker, k3, p6, k3, sl marker, purl to end.

Rows 2, 4, 6 (RS): Knit to marker, sl marker, p3, k6, p3, sl marker, knit to end.

Row 8: Knit to marker, sl marker, p3, C6B, p3, sl marker, knit to end.

Rows 9, 11, 13 and 15: Rep Row 1.

Rows 10, 12 and 14: Rep Row 2.

Row 16: Knit to marker, sl marker, p3, C6F, p3, sl marker, knit to end.

Continue in pat as established until right sleeve measures same as left sleeve.

Bind off.

Finishing
Block pieces to finished measurements.

Bind off shoulders tog using 3-Needle Bind-Off (see page 26), leaving centre back 32 (36, 40, 40, 44) sts on needle.

Collar
With RS facing and smaller needle, beg at left shoulder, pick up and knit 44 (44, 47, 49, 49) sts along left neck edge, knit centre front 16 (18, 20, 20, 22) sts, pick up and knit 44 (44, 47, 49, 49) sts along right neck edge, then knit across centre back 32 (36, 40, 40, 44) sts, place marker for beg of rnd and join. (136, 142, 154, 158, 164 sts)

Knit 6 rnds.

Bind off.

Sew on sleeves
With RS facing and using Invisible Seam (see page 24), sew sleeve seam from cast-on edge to markers.

With RS facing and using Invisible Seam, sew sleeve seams from markers to top.

Weave in all ends. ■

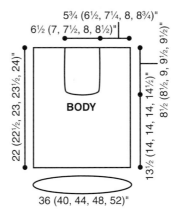

5¾ (6½, 7¼, 8, 8¾)"
6½ (7, 7½, 8, 8½)"
22 (22½, 23, 23½, 24)"
8½ (8½, 9, 9½, 9½)"
13½ (14, 14, 14, 14½)"
BODY
36 (40, 44, 48, 52)"

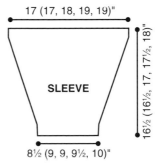

17 (17, 18, 19, 19)"
16½ (16½, 17, 17½, 18)"
SLEEVE
8½ (9, 9, 9½, 10)"

CUDDLY BABY BUNTING

Baby will be both stylish and toasty in a bunting with attached hood.

Design by Kennita Tully

Skill Level
INTERMEDIATE

Sizes
Infant's 0–3 (3–6, 6–9, 9–12) months. Instructions are given for smallest size, with larger sizes in parentheses. When only 1 number is given, it applies to all sizes.

Finished Measurements
Chest: 22 (24, 25½, 27) inches
Length: 22 (23, 24, 25) inches

Materials
Sock weight yarn (230 yds/50g per ball):
  3 (3, 4, 4) balls sea blues
Size 2 (2.75mm) double-pointed needles and
  16-inch circular needle
Size 3 (3.25mm) double-pointed needles, 16- and 24-
  inch circular needles or size needed to obtain gauge
Stitch markers
Stitch holders
Tapestry needle
4 (5, 5, 6) hook-and-loop tape dots

SUPER FINE

Gauge
27 sts and 32 rows = 4 inches/10cm in St st with
  larger needles
To save time, take time to check gauge.

Hem
Make 2

With smaller 16-inch circular needle, cast on 75 (81, 87, 91) sts.

Work even in St st for ¾ inch. Change to larger needles and work even for ¾ inch more.

With smaller needles, pick up each cast-on st. Fold hem in half, having WS tog.

Next row (RS): With needles held parallel, insert RH needle in first st of front and back needles, k2tog. Continue joining sts of both needles, by working k2tog to end of row.

Place sts on holder. Make 2nd hem, leave sts on needle.

Join for body
Knit across sts on holder, place marker, knit to end of rnd. Join, place marker between first and last st. (150, 162, 174, 182 sts)

Work even in St st until body measures 16½ (17, 17½, 18) inches.

Place all sts on holder.

Cuddly Baby Bunting
Sample project was knit with
Forever Jacquard (75 per cent
wool/25 per cent polyamide)
from Plymouth Yarn Co.

Sleeves

With smaller dpns, cast on 38 (38, 42, 44) sts.

Knit 6 rnds, change to larger needles and knit 6 more rnds.

Fold hem in half and join as for body.

Next rnd: Knit, inc 4 sts evenly. (42, 42, 46, 48 sts)

Knit 3 rnds.

[Inc 1 st each side of marker every 4th rnd] 3 (9, 5, 6) times, then [every 6th (0, 6th, 6th] rnd 4 (0, 4, 4) times. (56, 60, 64, 68 sts)

Work even until sleeve measures 5 (5½, 6, 6½) inches.

Knit 1 rnd, ending 6 (6, 7, 7) sts before marker.

Place 12 (12, 14, 14) sts on holder, place rem sts on 2nd holder.

Yoke
Joining sleeves & body
K63 (69, 73, 77) sts for front, place next 12 (12, 14, 14) sts on holder for underarm, k44 (48, 50, 54) sts for right sleeve, k63 (69, 73, 77) sts for back, place next 12 (12, 14, 14) sts on holder for underarm, k44 (48, 50, 54) sleeve sts. Place marker between first and last st. (214, 234, 246, 262 sts)

Mark joining rnd.

Work even until yoke measures 2¾ (3, 3¼, 3½) inches above marker.

Dec rnd: *K1, k2tog; rep from * around. (144, 156, 164, 176 sts)

Work even until yoke measures 4¼ (4½, 4¾, 5) inches above marker.

Rep Dec Rnd. (96, 104, 112, 120 sts)

Work even until yoke measures 5½ (6, 6½, 7) inches above marker.

Rep Dec Rnd. (64, 72, 76, 80 sts)

Hood
Removing previous markers, mark centre front.

Knit to marker st, turn, purl to end of rnd.

Work in rows from this point.

Next row (RS): Knit, inc 13 (11, 13, 15) sts. (77, 83, 89, 95 sts)

Work even in St st until hood measures 6 inches, ending with a RS row.

Next row: P38 (41, 44, 47), purl next st and mark it, purl to end of row.

Shape back
[Knit to 2 sts before marked st, ssk, k1, k2tog, Purl 1 row] 4 times. (69, 75, 81, 87 sts)

Next row (WS): Dec 1 st at centre of hood.

Finishing
Fold hood in half and join top seam using Kitchener Stitch (see page 24).

Sew underarm seam in same manner.

Sew 4 (5, 5, 6) hook-and-loop tape dots to bottom hem of bunting. ∎

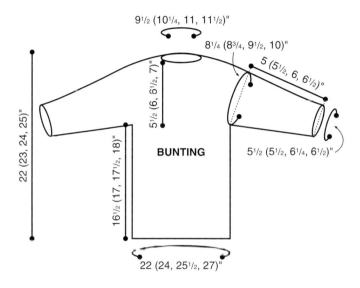

9½ (10¼, 11, 11½)"

8¼ (8¾, 9½, 10)"

5 (5½, 6, 6½)"

5½ (6, 6½, 7)"

22 (23, 24, 25)"

16½ (17, 17½, 18)"

BUNTING

5½ (5½, 6¼, 6½)"

22 (24, 25½, 27)"

BABY FLUFF

A classic baby set, trimmed with chic bands of pastel fluff, is a perfect gift for a special baby.

Designs by Lainie Hering

Skill Level

INTERMEDIATE

Sizes

Infant's 0–3 (6–9, 12–18) months. Instructions are given for smallest size, with larger sizes in parentheses. When only 1 number is given, it applies to all sizes.

Finished Measurement

Sweater chest: 22 (23, 24) inches

Materials

Worsted weight yarn (200 yds/100g per skein):
   3 skeins off-white (MC)
Novelty yarn (55 yds/50g per ball):
   1 ball white/gold (CC)
Size 6 (4mm) needles
Size 7 (4.5mm) 16-inch circular needle
Size 8 (5mm) double-pointed needles, 16- and 24-inch
   circular needles or size needed to obtain gauge
1 (¾-inch) button
1 yd (⅜-inch) off-white double-faced satin ribbon
Stitch markers
Stitch holders

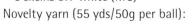

Gauge

18 sts and 25 rnds = 4 inches/10cm in St st with MC and size 8 needles

To save time, take time to check gauge.

Special Abbreviation

M1 (Make 1): With LH needle, lift strand between last st worked and next st on LH needle, and knit into back of it.

Pm: Place marker.

Pattern Stitches

Seed Stitch (worked in rnds)

Rnd 1: *K1, p1; rep from * around.

Rnd 2: *P1, k1; rep from * around.

Rep Rnds 1–2 for pat.

Seed Stitch (worked in rows)

All rows: *K1, p1; rep from * across.

Stripe Sequence

Knit 3 rnds CC, 4 (5, 5) rnds MC, 3 rnds CC.

Pattern Note

Sweater is worked from the neck downward.

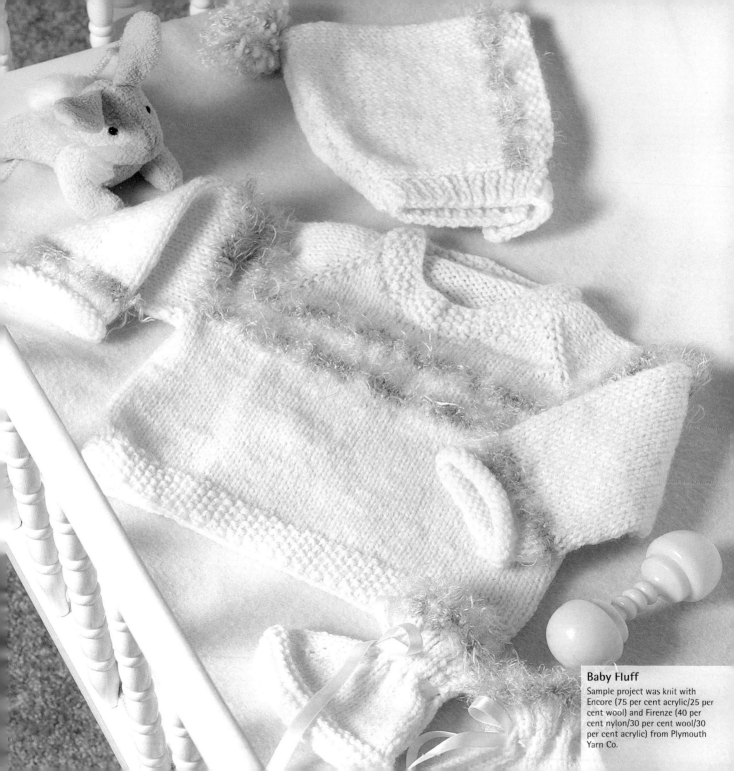

Baby Fluff
Sample project was knit with Encore (75 per cent acrylic/25 per cent wool) and Firenze (40 per cent nylon/30 per cent wool/30 per cent acrylic) from Plymouth Yarn Co.

Sweater

Beg at neck with MC and largest needle, cast on 36 sts. Do not join.

Set-up row (RS): K1, pm, k1 (seam st), pm, k6 (sleeve), pm, k1 (seam st), pm, k18 (back), pm, k1 (seam st), pm, k6 (sleeve), pm, k1 (seam st), pm, k1.

Purl 1 row.

Begin neck shaping
Inc row 1: *K to marker, M1, sl marker, knit seam st, sl marker, M1; rep from * 3 times, knit to end of row. (44 sts)

Purl 1 row.

Inc row 2: Continue to inc at markers as before, *at the same time* inc 1 st in each end st by knitting into the front and back of st.

Purl 1 row.

[Rep last 2 rows] 3 times. (84 sts)

Join for yoke
Next row: Rep inc row 1, cast on 8 sts at end of row, join and knit to first marker. (100 sts)

Marker between front and right sleeve will now denote beg of rnd.

Begin stripe
Beg stripe pat when there are 32 (34, 34) sts on front, *at the same time* continue to inc at markers [every other rnd] 3 (5, 6) times, then [every 4th rnd] once. (132, 148, 156 sts)

Work even until yoke measures 5 (5½, 6) inches when measured at centre back.

Divide work
Sl sts onto 4 separate holders as follows: 26 (30, 32) sts for each sleeve, 38 (42, 44) back or front sts plus 2 seam sts.

Sleeves
Next rnd: With size 8 dpns, cast on 4 sts, k26 (30, 32) sleeve sts from holder, cast on 4 sts, divide sts among dpns, pm between first and last st. (34, 38, 40 sts)

Working in St st, [dec 1 st each side of marker every 8th (6th, 7th) rnd] 3 (4, 4) times. (28, 30, 32 sts)

Work even until sleeve measures 4½ (5, 5½) inches.

Knit 3 rnds in CC.

Change to MC and work even until sleeve measures 6 (6½, 7) inches.

Bind off.

Body

Sl front and back sts from holders to size 8 circular needle. Mark this rnd.

Cast on 4 sts, knit front sts, cast on 4 sts, pm, cast on 4 sts, knit back sts, cast on 4 sts, pm to denote beg of rnd.

Work even until body measures 4½ (5½, 6) inches above marker.

Change to size 7 needles.

Work even in Seed St for 1 inch.

Bind off in pat.

Neck Band

With MC and size 7 needle, pick up and knit 60 sts around neck edge.

Work even in Seed St for ¾ (1, 1) inch.

Bind off in pat.

Sew underarm seam, using Kitchener Stitch (see page 24).

Hat

Hem

With MC and size 7 needle, cast on 57 (61, 65) sts.

Work in Seed St for 1 inch. Change to size 8 needle.

With CC, work 4 rows St st. Cut CC, join MC.

Body

Work even until hat measures 4½ (5, 5½) inches, ending with a WS row.

[Dec 1 st each end every row] 6 times. (45, 49, 53 sts)

Bind off 5 sts at beg of next 4 rows.

Bind off rem 25 (29, 33) sts.

Fold hood in half and sew back seam.

Neck Band
With RS facing and size 7 needle pick up and knit 38 (40, 44) sts evenly around lower edge of hat, cast on 11 (11, 13) sts. (49, 51, 57 sts)

Work even in k1, p1 rib for 7 rows making buttonhole on Row 4.

Buttonhole row (RS): Work in pat to last 4 sts, yo, k2tog, p1, k1.

Bind off in pat.

Finishing
Sew on button.

Make a small pompom using 1 strand each of MC and CC held tog (see page 80).

Sew pompom to point of hat.

Booties

With CC and size 6 needle, cast on 32 sts.

Knit 1 row, purl 1 row. Change to MC.

Work even in k2, p2 rib for 8 (8, 10) rows.

Eyelet row: K1, *yo, k2tog; rep from * across, end last rep k1.

Next row: P14, pm, p4, pm, p14.

Inc row: Knit to 1 st before marker, M1, k1, knit to next marker, k1, M1, knit to end of row.

Purl 1 row.

[Rep last 2 rows] 5 (6, 6) times. (44, 46, 46 sts)

Size 12–18 months only: Knit 1 row, purl 1 row.

All sizes: Work even in garter st for 8 (9, 10) rows.

Bind off.

Finishing
Sew sole and back of bootie.

Cut ribbon to measure 18 inches and weave through eyelet row. ■

TUTTI-FRUTTI TOP

Colourful variegated stripes and easy-care cotton highlight a girl's summery top.

Design by Bonnie Franz

Skill Level

EASY

Sizes
Child's 4 (6, 8, 10) Instructions are given for smallest size, with larger sizes in parentheses. When only 1 number is given, it applies to all sizes.

Finished Measurements
Chest: 27 (28½, 30, 34) inches
Length: 15½ (16½, 19, 20) inches

Materials
Worsted weight yarn (140 yds/100g per ball):
  3 (3, 3, 4) balls each lime (MC) and orange variegated (CC)
Size 8 (5mm) double-pointed needles, 16- and 24-inch circular needles or size needed to obtain gauge
Stitch markers
Stitch holder
Tapestry needle

4 MEDIUM

Gauge
18 sts and 18 rows = 4 inches/10cm in colour pat
To save time, take time to check gauge.

Pattern Stitch
Diagonal Stripe (multiple of 6 sts + 5)

Rnd 1: *K3 MC, k3 CC; rep from *, end last rep k2 CC.

Rnd 2: *K1 CC, k3 MC, k2 CC; rep from *, end last rep k1 CC.

Rnd 3: *K2 CC, k3 MC, k1 CC; rep from *, end last rep k3 MC.

Rnd 4: *K3 CC, k3 MC; rep from *, end last rep k2 MC.

Rnd 5: *K1 MC, k3 CC, k2 MC; rep from *, end last rep k1 MC.

Rnd 6: *K2 MC, k3 CC, k1 MC; rep from *, end last rep k3 CC.

Rep Rnds 1–6 for pat.

Body
With MC and longer needle, cast on 60 (62, 66, 74) sts, place marker, cast on 59 (63, 65, 75) sts. Join without twisting, place marker between first and last st.

[Knit 1 round, purl 1 round] 3 times.

Work even in Diagonal Stripe pat until body measures 9½ (10, 12, 12) inches.

Divide for front & back
Work in pat to first marker and place sts on holder.

Work in rows from this point.

Back

Work even in established pat on rem 59 (63, 65, 75) sts until armhole measures 6 (6½, 7, 8) inches.

Bind off all sts.

Front

Sl sts from holder to needle.

With RS facing, join yarns at left armhole.

Work even in established pat until armhole measures 2½ (2½, 3, 3) inches, ending with a WS row.

Shape neck

Next row: Work across 22 (24, 24, 29) sts, place rem sts on hold.

[Dec 1 st at neck edge every other row] 5 (6, 5, 6) times. (17, 18, 19, 23 sts)

Work even until armhole measures same as for back.

Bind off all sts.

With RS facing, join yarns at left edge of neck.

Next row: Bind off 16 (14, 18, 16) sts, work to end of row.

Work RS of neck as for left, reversing shaping.

Sew shoulder seams.

Sleeves

With MC and shorter circular needle (or dpns), pick up and knit 54 (58, 64, 72) sts around armhole. Join, place marker between first and last st.

Beg colour pat as given for body.

Maintaining pat as much as possible, [dec 1 st each side of marker every 4th rnd] 0 (0, 2, 7) times, then [every 3rd rnd] 10 (12, 12, 10) times, and finally [every 2nd rnd] 1 (0, 0, 0) time. (32, 34, 36, 38 sts)

Work even until sleeve measures 9¼ (10¼, 11¾, 12¾) inches.

With MC, [knit 1 row, purl 1 row] twice.

Bind off.

Finishing

With MC and shorter circular needle, pick up and knit 64 (66, 72, 70) sts around neck edge.

[Knit 1 row, purl 1 row] twice.

Bind off loosely. ■

Tutti-Frutti Top
Sample project was knit with
Fantasy Naturale (100 per
cent mercerized cotton) from
Plymouth Yarn Co.

LITTLE MISS PRECIOUS

Here's a dressy poncho for a young sugar 'n' spice girl. Change the ribbon for everyday wear!

Design by Kennita Tully

Skill Level
INTERMEDIATE

Finished Measurements
Circumference at lower edge: Approx 42 inches
Length: 7½ inches

Materials
Worsted weight yarn (76½ yds/50g per skein):
  3 skeins pink

Size 5 (3.75mm) 16-inch circular needle
Size 8 (5mm) 24-inch circular needle or size needed
  to obtain gauge
Large-eye tapestry needle
Stitch markers
Approx 3½ yds ribbon

Gauge
18 sts and 24 rows = 4 inches/10cm in St st with larger
  needles
To save time, take time to check gauge.

Pattern Notes
For Make 1 Right (M1R) and Make 1 Left (M1L) incs, refer
to Special Techniques on page 26.

Neck Band
With smaller needle, cast on 80 sts. Join without twisting,
mark beg of rnd.

Rnds 1–3: Knit around.

Rnd 4 (eyelet rnd): *K3, yo, k2tog; rep from * around.

Rnds 5 and 6: Knit around.

Rnd 7 (turning ridge): Purl around.

Rnds 8 and 9: Knit around.

Rnd 10 (eyelet rnd): Rep Rnd 4.

Rnds 11–13: Knit around.

Begin raglan shaping
Change to larger circular needle and knit 1 rnd, placing
markers for raglan shaping: K13, place marker, k14, place
marker, k26, place marker, k14, place marker, k13. Do not
remove marker at beg of rnd.

Rnd 1: *Knit to 1 st before raglan marker, M1R, k1, sl
marker, k1, M1L; rep from * around. (88 sts)

Rnd 2: Knit around.

Rep Rnds 1 and 2 until 9 inc rnds have been completed.
(152 sts)

When raglan shaping is completed, work even until topper measures 3 inches from last inc rnd or ½ inch less than desired length.

Eyelet Border

Rnd 1: *K1, p1; rep from * around.

Rnd 2 (eyelet rnd): Working in seed st (purl the knit sts and knit the purl sts), *[p1, k1] twice, yo, k2tog; rep from * until 14 sts rem, end [p1, k1] twice, p1, yo, p2tog, [k1, p1] twice, k1, yo, k2tog.

Beg with a knit st, bind off all sts in seed st.

Finishing

Fold neck band to inside along turning ridge. Matching eyelets in underside of neck band to eyelets on outside of neck band, neatly sew neck band facing to inside of topper. Use a loose tension on sewing yarn so neck band will retain its stretch.

Block as desired.

Thread ribbon into a large-eyed tapestry needle. Referring to photo, beg off-centre and weave ribbon in and out of eyelets in neck band. Tie bow and trim ribbon ends. Rep at bottom edge. ∎

Little Miss Precious
Sample project was knit with Filatura di Crosa Primo (100 per cent merino wool) from Tahki/ Stacy Charles.

BUSY DAY DRESS

Playful little girls will enjoy wearing this clever knit dress alone or over a T-shirt—it's simply darling.

Design by Joyce Nordstrom

Skill Level

EASY

Sizes

Child's sizes 2 (6) Instructions are given for smaller size, with larger size in parentheses. When only 1 number is given, it applies to both sizes.

Finished Measurements

Chest: 22½ (26½) inches
Length: 16 (17½) inches

Materials

Light weight yarn (147 yd/50g per ball):
  3 (4) balls pink/blue/yellow multicolour
Size 4 (3.5mm) double-pointed needles
Size 6 (4mm) 24-inch circular needle or size needed to obtain gauge
Stitch markers, 1 in CC for beg of rnd
Tapestry needle

Gauge

20 sts and 28 rows = 4 inches/10cm in St st with larger needles
To save time, take time to check gauge.

Pattern Note

Sundress is worked from shoulders down to underarms; front and back are then joined and worked in the round to bottom.

Back Yoke

With larger circular needle, cast on 40 (48) sts. Do not join.

Work even in St st for 3½ (4) inches, ending with a WS row.

Inc 1 st at each armhole edge on next, then [every other row] 1 (2) more time(s), ending with a WS row. (44, 54 sts)

Cast on 2 sts at beg of next 6 rows. (56, 66 sts)

Sl all sts to waste yarn.

Front Yoke & Neck

With RS facing and using larger needle, pick up and knit 10 (12) sts along cast-on edge of back; skip centre 20 (24) back neck sts; with 2nd ball, pick up and knit rem 10 (12) sts.

Working both sides at once with separate balls of yarn, work 3 rows of St st.

Inc 1 st at each neck edge [every RS row] 7 (9) times, ending with a WS row. (17, 21 sts on each side)

Cut yarn on left front.

Work across right front sts, cast on 6 sts, then work across left front sts. (40, 48 sts)

Work even until front measures 3½ (4) inches, ending with a WS row.

Inc 1 st at each armhole edge on next, then [every other row] 1 (2) more time(s), ending with a WS row. (44, 54 sts)

Cast on 2 sts at beg of next 6 rows. (56, 66 sts)

Body
Rnd 1 (RS): Knit across front sts, place marker, sl back sts from waste yarn to LH needle and knit across, place marker for beg of rnd and join. (112, 132 sts)

Knit 8 rnds even.

Inc rnd: *K1, M1, knit to 1 st before marker, M1, k1, sl marker; rep from * to end of rnd. (116, 136 sts)

Rep Inc rnd [every 9th rnd] 6 (7) times. (140, 164 sts)

Work even until body measures approx 10 (10¾) inches from armholes or 1 inch short of desired length.

Work in k2, p2 rib for 1 inch.

Bind off loosely in rib.

Finishing
Armhole edging
With RS facing, using smaller dpns and beg at centre underarm, pick up and knit 56 (60) sts around armhole edge, place marker for beg of rnd and join.

Work 4 rnds in k2, p2 rib.

Bind off very loosely in rib.

Neck edging
With RS facing and using dpns, pick up and knit 60 (68) sts around neck edge.

Work as for armhole edging.

Weave in all ends. Block to finished measurements. ■

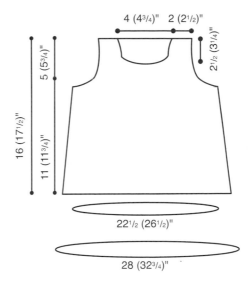

SHADES FOR PLAY

Colour progression stripes, a rolled-edge trim and an easy raglan increase technique make this pullover quick as well as easy!

Design by Sara Louise Harper

Skill Level

Sizes

Child's 4 (6, 8, 10, 12) Instructions are given for smallest size, with larger sizes in parentheses. When only 1 number is given, it applies to all sizes.

Finished Measurements

Chest: 28 (30, 32, 34, 36) inches
Length: 14¾ (16, 17¼, 17¾, 19) inches, excluding collar

Materials

Worsted weight yarn (210 yds/100g per ball):
  1 (1, 1, 2, 2) ball(s) each light teal (A), light blue (B) and medium blue (C)
Size 8 (5mm) double-pointed needles and 29-inch circular needle or size needed to obtain gauge
Stitch markers
Tapestry needle

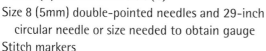

Gauge

16 sts and 24 rows = 4 inches/10cm in St st
To save time, take time to check gauge.

Special Abbreviations

M1L (Make 1 Left): Insert LH needle from front to back under the running thread between the last st worked and next st on LH needle. With RH needle, knit into the back of the resulting lp.

M1R (Make 1 Right): Insert LH needle from back to front under running thread between the last st worked and next st on LH needle. With RH needle, knit into the front of the resulting lp.

Pm: Place marker.

Pattern Stitch
Colour Progression

*Knit 1 rnd with new colour, then 1 rnd with old colour; rep from * once, then continue with new colour.

Pattern Notes

This raglan sweater is worked down from the rolled collar. When the yoke is complete, sleeve stitches are placed on waste yarn while the body is completed; sleeves are worked in the round from the armhole down.

When measuring the final length, allow edge to roll slightly as it will when worn.

The M1 raglan stitches are both worked in the same running thread; the 2nd will be tight to work.

Rolled Collar

With circular needle and A, cast on 72 (74, 76, 78, 78) sts, pm and join, being careful not to twist sts.

Shades for Play
Sample project was knit with Galway Worsted (100 per cent wool) from Plymouth Yarn Co.

Work in St st for 2 inches. Pm in the fabric on last rnd.

Yoke

Set-up rnd: Knit around, placing markers as follows: 22 (24, 26, 28, 30) front sts, pm; 14 (13, 12, 11, 9) sleeve sts,

pm, 22 (24, 26, 28, 30) back sts, pm; 14 (13, 12, 11, 9) sleeve sts.

Raglan Inc rnd: *Knit to marker, M1L, sl marker, M1R; rep from * to beg of rnd marker, making last M1R following that marker.

Rep Raglan Inc rnd [every other rnd] 16 (17, 18, 19, 20) times. (208, 218, 228, 238, 246 sts)

At the same time, when 25 (27, 29, 31, 33) rnds have been worked from the marker, change to B and beg working the Colour Progression pat.

Separate Body & Sleeves

When raglan incs are complete, place 48 (49, 50, 51, 51) sleeve sts on waste yarn.

Body

Continue working 112 (120, 128, 136, 144) body sts in St st and *at the same time*, when 25 (27, 29, 31, 33) rnds of B are complete, change to C and work Colour Progression pat again.

Continue in C until body measures 9 (10, 11, 11, 12) inches or desired length from underarm.

Bind off all sts very loosely, allowing lower edge to roll.

Sleeves

Sl sleeve sts to dpns, then pick up and knit 2 sts from underarm, placing beg of rnd marker between them. (50, 51, 52, 53, 53 sts)

Work 3 (3, 4, 4, 6) rnds even in St st.

Dec rnd: K1, ssk, knit to last 3 sts, k2tog, k1. (48, 49, 50, 51, 51 sts)

Continue in St st and rep Dec rnd [every 4th (4th, 5th, 5th, 7th) rnd] 11 (11, 11, 11, 10) times. (26, 27, 28, 29, 31 sts)

At the same time, when 25 (27, 29, 31, 33) rnds of B are complete, change to C and work Colour Progression pat again.

Work even until sleeve measures 8 (9, 10, 11, 12) inches or desired length.

Bind off very loosely, allowing cuff to roll.

Finishing
Weave in loose ends. Block to finished measurements. ■

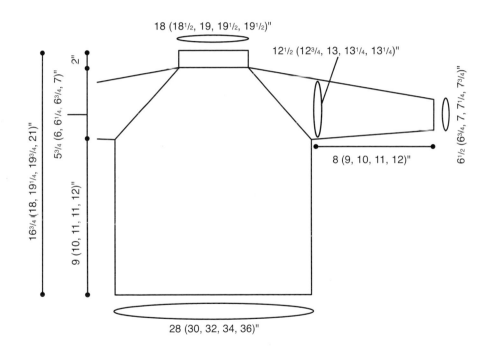

18 (18½, 19, 19½, 19½)"

12½ (12¾, 13, 13¼, 13¼)"

2"

5¾ (6, 6¼, 6¾, 7)"

16¾ (18, 19¼, 19¾, 21)"

9 (10, 11, 11, 12)"

6½ (6¾, 7, 7¼, 7¾)"

8 (9, 10, 11, 12)"

28 (30, 32, 34, 36)"

ANGEL BABY

Citrus and confetti-like colours combine
in a dress fit for an angel.

Design by Barbara Venishnick

Skill Level
EASY

Sizes
Child's 2 (4, 6, 8) Instructions are given for smallest size, with larger sizes in parentheses. When only 1 number is given, it applies to all sizes.

Finished Measurements
Chest: 23 (25, 27, 29) inches
Length: 15¾ (17¾, 19¾, 21¾) inches

Materials
DK weight yarn (126 yds/50g per ball):
   3 (4, 5, 6) balls citrus multicolour (MC)
Novelty eyelash yarn (190 yds/50g per ball):
   1 ball lime (CC)
Size 6 (4mm) 16-, 24- and 29-inch circular
   needles or size needed to obtain gauge
Size D/3 (3.25mm) crochet hook
Stitch markers
Stitch holder

Gauge
20 sts and 30 rnds = 4 inches/10cm with MC in St st
To save time, take time to check gauge.

Dress
With longest needle and MC, cast on 160 (172, 184, 196)

sts. Join without twisting, place marker between first and last st.

Work even in St st for 1½ inches.

Purl 1 rnd for turning rnd.

Change to CC and knit 1 rnd.

Work even in rev St st for 1½ inches. Change to MC and knit 1 rnd, place marker after every 40th (43rd, 46th, 49th) st.

Dec rnd: [Knit to marker, k2tog] 4 times.

Knit 4 (5, 5, 6) rnds.

[Rep these 5 (6, 6, 7) rnds] 11 times, changing to shorter needles when necessary. (112, 124, 136, 148 sts)

Work even until dress measures 10 (11½, 13, 14½) inches above turning rnd.

Divide work
Place last 56 (62, 68, 74) sts worked on holder for front.

Work in rows from this point.

Angel Baby
Sample project was knit with
Dreambaby Kokonut (67 per cent
acrylic/33 per cent nylon) and
Flash (100 per cent nylon) from
Plymouth Yarn Co.

Back

Bind off 3 sts at beg of the next 2 rows, then 2 sts at beg of following 2 rows.

[Dec 1 st each end every other row] 3 times. (40, 46, 52, 58 sts)

Work even until armhole measures 5 (5½, 6, 6½) inches, ending with a WS row.

Shape neck & shoulders

Next row (RS): K13 (15, 17, 19), join 2nd ball of yarn and bind off centre 14 (16, 18, 20) sts, k13 (15, 17, 19).

Working on both sides of neck with separate balls of yarn, [dec 1 st at each neck edge every other row] 3 times, *at the same time* bind off at each arm edge 3 (4, 5, 5) sts twice, then 4 (4, 4, 6) sts once.

Front

Work as for back until armhole measures 2½ (3, 3½, 4) inches, ending with a WS row.

Shape neck

Next row (RS): K13 (15, 17, 19), join 2nd ball of yarn and bind off centre 14 (16, 18, 20) sts, k13 (15, 17, 19).

[Dec 1 st at each side of neck every other row] 3 times. (10, 12, 14, 16 sts)

Work even until armhole measures same as for back.

Shape shoulders

Bind off at each arm edge 3 (4, 5, 5) sts twice, then 4 (4, 6) sts once.

Sew shoulder seams.

Neck Band

Beg at right shoulder with RS facing using shortest needle and CC, pick up and knit 8 sts along right neck edge, 14 (16, 18, 20) sts of back neck, 25 sts along left neck, 14 (16,

18, 20) sts of front neck, and 17 sts along right neck edge. Place marker between first and last st. (78 82, 86, 90 sts)

Work even in St st for 1½ inches.

Bind off very loosely, using a larger needle if desired.

Armhole Edging

With MC, work 1 rnd sc around entire armhole, making sure to keep work flat. Join with sl st, do not turn.

Working from left to right, work 1 sc in each sc of previous rnd.

Join with sl st, fasten off.

Rep around rem armhole. ■

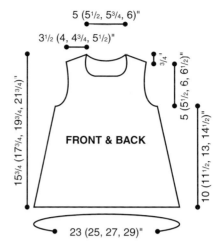

5 (5½, 5¾, 6)"

3½ (4, 4¾, 5½)"

¾"

5 (5½, 6, 6½)"

15¾ (17¾, 19¾, 21¾)"

FRONT & BACK

10 (11½, 13, 14½)"

23 (25, 27, 29)"

SCHOOL COLOURS SCARF & HAT

Fluffy pompoms adorn the ends of a scarf; the matching hat boasts a quirky topknot.

Designs by Uyvonne Bigham

Skill Level

BEGINNER

Size
One size fits most teens and adults

Finished Measurements
Scarf: 6½ x 60 inches
Hat circumference: 19 inches

Materials
Worsted weight yarn (200 yds/100g per skein):
   3 skeins hot pink (MC) and 1 skein off-
   white (CC)
Size 8 (5mm) double-pointed needles and 16-
   inch circular needle or size needed to obtain gauge
Stitch marker
4-inch piece of cardboard

Gauge
17 sts and 24 rnds = 4 inches/10cm in St st
To save time, take time to check gauge.

Hat

With MC and circular needle, cast on 80 sts. Join without twisting, place marker between first and last st.

Work even in St st until hat measures 26 inches.

Bind off.

Tie overhand knot in top of hat.

Roll up cast-on edge.

**School Colours
Scarf & Hat**
Sample project was knit with
Encore (75 per cent acrylic/25
per cent wool) from Plymouth
Yarn Co.

Scarf

With MC and dpns, cast on 80 sts, leaving a 12-inch end for later sewing. Join without twisting, place marker between first and last st.

Work even in St st until scarf measures 3 inches.

Begin stripe pat
Work in stripe pat of 4 rnds CC, 5 rnds MC, 5 rnds CC.

Work even with MC only until scarf measures 55 inches.

Begin stripe pat
Work in stripe pat of 5 rnds CC, 5 rnds MC, 4 rnds CC.

Work even with MC only for 3 inches more.

Cut yarn, leaving a 12-inch end.

Finishing
Draw end through all sts twice and draw up tightly. Pull end to inside.

Rep along cast-on edge, running reserved end through all sts.

Pompoms
Make 2

Wind CC around cardboard approx 75 times. Tie 1 end, cut other end.

Shake pompom to fluff up.

Attach 1 pompom to each end of scarf. ■

ROLLED-BRIM HAT & MITTS

The use of stockinette stitch throughout this pair causes the edges to roll naturally.

Designs by Uyvonne Bigham

Skill Level
EASY

Size
Adult

Finished Measurements
Hat circumference: 17 inches
Mitten length: 9½ inches, with cuff unrolled

Materials
Worsted weight yarn (200 yds/100g per skein): **4** MEDIUM
   2 skeins blue/purple
Size 8 (5mm) double-pointed needles and 16-
   inch circular needle or size needed to obtain gauge
Stitch markers
Stitch holders

Gauge
19 sts and 26 rnds = 4 inches/10cm in St st
To save time, take time to check gauge.

Hat

Body
With circular needle, cast on 80 sts. Join without twisting, place marker between first and last st.

Work even in St st until hat measures 6 inches.

Shape top
Rnd 1: *K8, k2tog; rep from * around. (72 sts)

Rnd 2: Knit.

Rnd 3: *K7, k2tog; rep from * around. (64 sts)

Rnd 4: Knit.

Continue to dec every other rnd as established, having 1 st less between dec until 14 sts rem.

Knit 1 rnd.

Cut yarn leaving a 12-inch end. Draw yarn through rem sts twice. Pull tightly and secure.

Mittens
Make both alike

With dpns, cast on 32 sts. Join without twisting, place marker between first and last st.

Knit 40 rnds.

Thumb opening
Next rnd: K1, sl next 4 sts to holder, cast on 4 sts, knit to end of rnd.

Knit 38 rnds.

Mitten Top
Rnd 1: [Ssk, k12, k2tog] twice. (28 sts)

Rnd 2 and all even-numbered rnds: Knit.

Rnd 3: [Ssk, k10, k2tog] twice. (24 sts)

Rnd 5: [Ssk, k8, k2tog] twice. (20 sts)

Rnd 7: [Ssk, k6, k2tog] twice. (16 sts)

Rnd 9: [Ssk, k4, k2tog] twice. (12 sts)

Knit 1 rnd.

Rearrange sts so there are 6 sts on each of 2 needles, having a dec st at each end of needle.

Sew sts tog, using Kitchener Stitch (see page 24).

Thumb
Pick up and knit 10 sts around thumb opening. Divide onto 3 needles.

Work even in St st for 1½ inches.

Next rnd: *K2tog around.

Cut yarn leaving a 6-inch end.

Draw yarn through rem sts twice. Pull tightly and secure.

Press thumbs to right or left for appropriate mitten. ■

Rolled-Brim Hat & Mitts
Sample project was knit with Encore Colorspun (75 per cent acrylic/25 per cent wool) from Plymouth Yarn Co.

QUICK UNISEX HATS

Start at the top and end with earflaps using chunky yarn in colourful prints or sensible solid shades.

Design by Cecily Glowik

Skill Level
EASY

Sizes
Woman's (man's) Instructions are given for smaller size, with larger size in parentheses. When only 1 number is given, it applies to both sizes.

Finished Measurement
Head circumference: 20 (22) inches

Materials
Super bulky weight yarn (49 yds/50g per ball):
   2 balls pastels multicolour [woman's hat]
Super bulky weight yarn (51 yds/100g per skein):
   2 skeins dark blue [man's hat]
Size 17 (12.75mm) double-pointed needles and
   16-inch circular needle (optional) or size needed
   to obtain gauge
Stitch marker
Tapestry needle

Gauge
8 sts and 10 rnds = 4 inches/10cm in St st
To save time, take time to check gauge.

Special Abbreviations
Inc1 (Increase 1): Inc by knitting in front and back of st.

M1 (Make 1): Insert LH needle from front to back under the running thread between the last st worked and next st on LH. With RH needle, knit into the back of resulting lp.

Special Technique
I-Cord: *Sl sts back to LH needle, k3, do not turn; rep from * until cord is desired length. Bind off.

Pattern Stitch
Seed St in the Rnd (even number of sts)

Rnd 1: *K1, p1; rep from * around.

Rnd 2: *P1, k1; rep from * around.

Rep Rnds 1 and 2 for pat.

Pattern Note
If desired, change to 16-inch circular needle when stitches will fit comfortably on it.

Body
Cast on 3 sts onto 1 dpns, then distribute onto 3 dpns (1 st on each needle); place marker for beg of rnd and join, being careful not to twist sts.

Rnd 1: [Inc1] around. (6 sts)

Rnds 2, 5, 7, 9: Knit.

Quick Unisex Hats

Sample woman's hat was knit with Action (70 per cent acrylic/30 per cent wool) from N.Y. Yarns.

Sample man's hat was knit with Aspen (50 per cent alpaca/50 per cent wool) from Classic Elite Yarns.

Rnd 3: *K1, M1, k1; rep from * around. (9 sts)

Rnd 4: *K1, M1, k1, m1, k1; rep from * around. (15 sts)

Rnd 6: *K2, M1; rep from * to last st, k1. (22 sts)

Rnd 8: *K3, M1; rep from * to last st, k1. (29 sts)

Rnd 10: *K4, M1; rep from * to last st, k1. (36 sts)

Rnd 11: Knit all sts.

Rnd 12: Inc 0 (4) sts evenly spaced around. (36, 40 sts)

Rnds 13–18: Knit.

Rnds 19–24 (26): Work in Seed St.

Next rnd: Bind off 3 (4) sts, k9 sts and sl sts to waste yarn for earflap, bind off 12 (14) sts, k9 sts and sl to waste yarn for 2nd earflap, bind off rem 3 (4) sts.

Earflaps
Sl 9 sts from waste yarn to dpns and attach yarn with WS facing.

Rows 1, 3 and 5 (WS): Purl.

Rows 2 and 4: Sl 1, ssk, knit to last 3 sts, k2tog, sl 1. (5 sts)

Row 6: Sl 1, k3tog, sl 1, do not turn. (3 sts)

Work 3-st I-Cord for 7 inches.

K3tog and pull yarn through last st made.

Rep for 2nd earflap.

Finishing
Weave in ends. Block lightly. ◼

BERETS FOR MOM & DAUGHTER

The timeless beret is updated here in bright stripes.

Design by Lois S. Young

Skill Level

EASY

Sizes

Child's 2–4 (6–8, woman's) Instructions are given for smallest size, with larger sizes in parentheses. When only 1 number is given, it applies to all sizes.

Materials

Worsted weight yarn (245 yds/100g per skein)
  1 skein each pink (MC) and natural (CC)
Size 7 (4.5mm) set of double-pointed needles and 16-inch circular needle or size needed to obtain gauge
Stitch markers
Small piece of cardboard 2 (2, 3) inches wide for making pompom
8 (9¼, 10½)-inch-diameter plate or cardboard circle for blocking

Gauge

19 sts and 28 rows = 4 inches/10cm in pat
To save time, take time to check gauge.

Pattern Stitches

Stripe (size 2–4)

Rnd 1: With CC, knit.

Rnd 2: With CC, purl.

Rnds 3–9: With MC, knit.

Rep Rnds 1–9 for pat.

Stripe (size 6–8)

Rnd 1: With CC, knit.

Rnd 2: With CC, purl.

Rnds 3–10: With MC, knit.

Rep Rnds 1–10 for pat.

Stripe (woman's size)

Rnd 1: With CC, knit.

Rnd 2: With CC, purl.

Rnds 3–11: With MC, knit.

Rep Rnds 1–11 for pat.

Pattern Notes

Amounts given will make 1 child and 1 adult hat.

Change to double-pointed needles when hat circumference becomes too small for circular needle.

Beret must be blocked to shape. To block, dampen and stretch over large dinner plate or cardboard circle; let dry.

Beret

With circular needle and MC, cast on 75 (84, 90) sts. Join without twisting, marking beg of rnd.

Border
Knit 7 (8, 9) rnds. Work Rnds 1 and 2 of Stripe pat in CC for turning ridge. [Knit 3 (3, 4) rnds in MC, work Rnds 1 and 2 of Stripe pat in CC] twice.

Body
Work Rnds 3–9 (3–10, 3–11) of Stripe pat, working Rnd 4 as an inc rnd: *K2, [k1, p1] in next st; rep from * around. (100, 112, 120 sts)

Work Rnds 1–9 (1–10, 1–11) of Stripe pat, then work Rnds 1 and 2 (1–3, 1–4). On next rnd, dec 2 (0, 1) sts evenly. (98, 112, 119 sts)

Place markers every 14 (16, 17) sts for dec rnds.

Shape top
Maintaining established Stripe pat, dec on alternate rows by *working to 2 sts before marker, k2tog; rep from * around. When 7 sts are left, cut yarn, leaving a 6-inch end. Pull end through all sts, fasten off.

Turn border to inside on first CC ridge, sew in place for hem. Weave in ends, block.

Pompom
For instructions on making a pompom, see page 80. Make pompom with CC. Trim to spherical shape with diameter of 1½ (1¾, 2) inches.

Pull ends of ties to inside of hat, tie in knot. Do not weave in ends if you want to remove pompom when washing hat. ∎

Berets for Mom & Daughter

Sample project was knit with Nature Spun (100 per cent wool) from Brown Sheep Co.

SWEETHEART HAT

Textured heart panels brighten a hat sized for both adults and children.

Design by JoElyn Wheeler

Skill Level
EASY

Sizes
Child (adult) Instructions are given for smaller size, with larger size in parentheses. When only 1 number is given, it applies to both sizes.

Finished Measurement
Head circumference: 16 (20) inches

Materials
DK weight yarn (150 yds/50g per ball):
   1 (2) balls cranberry
Size 7 (4.5mm) 16-inch circular needle or size
   needed to obtain gauge
Stitch marker

Gauge
30 sts and 30 rnds = 4 inches/10cm in Heart pat
To save time, take time to check gauge.

Special Abbreviations
RT (Right Twist): Knit into front of 2nd st on LH needle, knit first st, sl both sts off needle.

LT (Left Twist): Knit into back of 2nd st on LH needle, knit first st, sl both sts off needle.

M1 (Make 1): With LH needle, pick up strand between st just worked and next st, knit into back of this st.

Pattern Stitch
Heart

Rnd 1: *K3, RT, LT, k3, p2, k1-tbl, p2; rep from * around.

Rnd 2 and all even-numbered rnds: *K10, p2, k1, p2; rep from * around.

Rnd 3: *K2, RT, k2, LT, k2, p2, k1-tbl, p2; rep from * around.

Rnd 5: *K1, RT, k4, LT, k1, p2, k1-tbl, p2; rep from * around.

Rnd 7: *RT, k6, LT, p2, k1-tbl, p2; rep from * around.

Rnd 9: Rep Rnd 1.

Rnd 11: *LT, RT, k2, LT, RT, p2, k1-tbl, p2; rep from * around.

Rnd 13: *K1, M1, K2tog-tbl, k4, k2tog, M1, k1, p2, k1-tbl, p2; rep from * around.

Rnd 15: *K10, p2, k1-tbl, p2; rep from * around.

Rnd 16: Rep Rnd 2.

Rep Rnds 1–16 for pat.

Sweetheart Hat
Sample project was knit with
Encore D.K. (75 per cent
acrylic/25 per cent wool) from
Plymouth Yarn Co.

Ribbing

Cast on 76 (92) sts. Join without twisting, place marker between first and last st.

Work even in k2, p2 ribbing for 3 inches, dec 1 (2) st(s) on last rnd. (75, 90 sts)

Body

Work Rnds 1–16 of Heart pat twice, then rep Rnds 1–12 once.

Shape crown

Rnd 1: *K1, k2tog-tbl, k4, k2tog, k1, p2, k1-tbl, p2; rep from * around. (65, 78 sts)

Rnd 2: *K8, p2, k1, p2; rep from * around.

Rnd 3: *K1, k2tog, k2, k2tog, k1, p2, k1-tbl, p2; rep from * around. (55, 66 sts)

Rnd 4: *K6, p2, k1, p2; rep from * around.

Rnd 5: *[K2tog] 3 times, p2tog, k1-tbl, p2tog; rep from * around. (30, 36 sts)

Rnd 6: *K3, p1, k1, p1; rep from * around.

Rnd 7: *Sl 1, k2tog, psso, p1, k1-tbl, p1; rep from * around. (20, 24 sts)

Rnd 8: K1, p1 around.

Rnd 9: K2tog around. (10, 12 sts)

Cut yarn, leaving a 12-inch end. Draw end through rem sts twice.

Pull tightly and fasten on inside.

Tassel

Cut 3 strands of yarn, each 18 inches long.

Pull strands through top of hat and adjust so ends are even.

Using 2 strands for each group, braid strands for 6 inches.

Tie ends of braid into a knot.

Cut 11 strands of yarn, each 9 inches long. Set 1 strand aside.

Centre 10 strands in rem yarn of braid. Tie braid ends around tassel strands.

Fold tassel strands in half and with rem strand of yarn, wrap strands tightly, ½ inch below fold.

Tie tightly, hiding all ends in tassel.

Trim tassel even. ■

JACQUARD HAT & GLITTENS

This versatile hand wear combines the dexterity of gloves with the warmth of mittens. The earflaps on the matching hat will keep chilly winds away.

Designs by Diane Elliott

Skill Level
INTERMEDIATE

Size
One size fits most adults

Materials
Sock weight yarn (230 yds/50g per ball): 2 balls blue/grey multi
Size 0 (2mm) double-pointed needles (2 only)
Size 2 (2.75mm) set of 5 double-pointed needles and 16-inch circular needle or size needed to obtain gauge
Size E/4 (3.5mm) crochet hook
Stitch markers
Stitch holders
Tapestry needle

Gauge
31 sts and 43 rnds = 4 inches/10cm in St st with larger needles
To save time, take time to check gauge.

Pattern Stitch
Mock Cable

Rnds 1 and 2: *K2, p2; rep from * around.

Rnd 3: *Knit 2nd st on LH needle leaving it on needle, knit first st on LH needle, sl both sts off, p2; rep from * around.

Rep Rnds 1–3 for pat.

Hat

Earflaps
Make 2

With larger needles, cast on 4 sts.

Rows 1 (RS) and 2: Knit.

Row 3: K1, inc in next st, knit to last 2 sts, inc in next st, k1.

Rows 4 and 6: Knit.

Rows 5 and 7: Rep Row 3.

Row 8: K3, purl to last 3 st, k3.

Rep Rows 7 and 8 until there are 20 sts.

Keeping first and last 3 sts in garter st, and rem sts in St st, work even until earflap measures 2½ inches.

Place sts on smaller dpns.

Hem
Beg at lower edge with larger circular needle, cast on 148

sts. Join without twisting, place marker between first and last st. Marker will be centre back of hat.

Next rnd: [K2, p2] 12 times, with RS facing, place 1 ear-flap behind work. Working in k2, p2 rib, work 1 st from main needle and 1 earflap st tog until all earflap sts have been joined. Work in rib over next 60 sts, join 2nd earflap as for first, work in rib to end of rnd.

Work even in Mock Cable pat for 1½ inches.

Body
Next rnd: Knit, inc 2 sts evenly. (150 sts)

Work even in St st until hat measures 5½ inches above cast-on edge.

Dec rnd: *K13, k2tog; rep from * around.

Knit 1 rnd.

Next rnd: *K12, k2tog; rep from * around.

Knit 1 rnd.

Continue to dec in this manner, having 1 less st between dec until 10 sts rem.

Cut yarn, leaving a 10-inch end.

Draw end through rem sts twice and pull tightly.

Braids
Cut 18 strands of yarn, each 24 inches long; separate into 3 sets of 6 strands each.

With crochet hook, pull 1 set through top of hat and adjust ends. Divide group into 3 strands of 4 each and braid tightly to approx 3 inches.

Tie an overhand knot in end.

Trim tassel to desired length.

Rep at bottom of each earflap with rem 2 sets of strands.

Glittens

With larger dpns, cast on 52 st. Divide evenly onto 4 needles. Join without twisting, place marker between first and last st.

Work even in Mock Cable pat for 2¾ inches.

Next rnd: Knit, inc 4 sts evenly. (56 sts)

Work even in St st until glitten measures 5½ inches, or desired length to thumb.

Begin thumb
Right glitten only: With a 12-inch strand of waste yarn, knit first 6 sts, drop waste yarn. Sl these 6 sts back to LH needle and knit them again with working yarn, knit to end of rnd.

Left glitten only: Knit to last 6 sts, k6 with waste yarn, drop waste yarn. Sl these 6 sts back to LH needle and knit them again with working yarn.

Both glittens: Work even for 1½ inches.

Begin finger
Work both glittens alike.

Jacquard Hat & Glittens
Sample project was knit with
Forever Jacquard (75 per cent
superwash wool/25 per cent
nylon) from Plymouth Yarn Co.

Next rnd: K6 and place on holder, knit to last 6 sts and place on 2nd holder. On following rnd, cast on 4 sts to last needle over held sts. (48 sts)

Knit 2 rnds.

Next rnd: Rearrange sts by slipping 2 sts of last needle to first needle. Mark new beg of rnd.

Work even until glitten measures 1¾ inch above 4 cast-on sts.

Dec rnd: *K6, k2tog; rep from * around. (42 sts)

Knit 4 rnds.

Dec rnd: *K5, k2tog; rep from * around. (36 sts)

Knit 4 rnds.

Dec rnd: *K4, k2tog; rep from * around. (30 sts)

Knit 4 rnds.

Dec rnd: *Sl 1, k2tog, psso; rep from * around. (10 sts)

Cut yarn, leaving a 10-inch end.

Draw end through rem sts twice and pull tightly.

Thumb

With smaller dpns and without removing waste yarn, pick up 6 sts on lower edge of thumb and 7 lps on upper edge. Remove contrast yarn.

With larger dpns, knit across 6 lower sts.

With 2nd needle, pick up and knit 2 sts along side of opening, then knit across 4 upper lps.

With 3rd needle, knit across rem 3 lps, pick up and knit 3 more sts along rem side of opening. (18 sts)

Work even in St st until thumb measures 2½ inches or desired length.

Dec rnd: *Sl 1, k2tog, psso; rep from * around. (9 sts)

Cut yarn, leaving a 10-inch end.

Draw end through rem sts twice and pull tightly.

Index Finger

Place st from first holder on 1 larger dpns. Attach yarn and knit these 6 sts onto first needle.

With 2nd needle, pick up and knit 1 st at side of opening, 4 sts along cast-on edge and 1 st at rem side of opening.

Place sts from 2nd holder on 3rd needle and knit them. (18 sts)

Mark first st on first needle as beg of rnd.

Work even in St st until finger measures 3 inches or desired length.

Dec rnd: *Sl 1, k2tog, psso; rep from * around. (9 sts)

Cut yarn, leaving a 10-inch end.

Draw end through rem sts twice and pull tightly. ■

SILLY HAT

*This warm and colourful topper will bring
a smile to any child's face.*

Design by Carol May

Skill Level
EASY

Size
Child's medium

Finished Measurements
Circumference: 16 inches
Length without tassel: 22 inches

Materials
Worsted weight yarn (200 yds/100g per ball):
  1 ball each purple (A), aqua (B), tan (C),
  burgundy (D), light rose (E) and blue/green
  multi (F)
Size 6 (4mm) double-pointed needles
Size 7 (4.5mm) double-pointed needles or size needed to
  obtain gauge
Stitch marker
Tapestry needle
5-inch-wide piece of stiff cardboard
Size H/8 (5mm) crochet hook

Gauge
26 sts and 34 rnds = 4 inches/10cm in Broken Stripes pat
  with larger needles
To save time, take time to check gauge.

Pattern Stitch
Broken Stripes

Rnds 1 and 2: *K3, sl 1; rep from * around.

Rnds 3 and 4: K1, *sl 1, k3; rep from * around.

Rep Rnds 1–4 for pat.

Work in colour sequence of 2 rnds each of: E, C, A, F, B, D, C, F, B, E, D, A.

Pattern Note
Carry colours not in use up work.

Ribbing
With A and smaller needles, cast on 120 sts.

Join without twisting, place marker between first and last st.

Work even in k2, p2 rib for 4 inches.

Next rnd: Knit, dec 16 sts evenly. (104 sts)

Body
Change to larger needles and E. Work even in Broken Stripes pat and colour sequence until hat measures 4 inches above ribbing.

Begin shaping
Dec rnd: K2tog, work to last 2 sts, ssk.

Work even for 3 rnds.

Working in established pat, rep these 4 rnds until 18 sts rem.

Next rnd: *K2tog; rep from * around. (9 sts)

Cut yarn and draw through rem sts twice.

Tassel
Cut a 16-inch length of A and set aside. Wrap A around cardboard approx 25 times. Tie 1 end with reserved length of yarn. Cut opposite end.

With another 16-inch length of A, wrap around tassel 3 times about 1 inch below first tie. Tie tightly and pull long ends into tassel to hide. Trim tassel even.

With crochet hook using 2 strands of first knot, ch 3, fasten off (see page 119).

Sew tassel to end of hat, weaving loose ends into inside. ■

Silly Hat
Sample project was knit with Encore (75 per cent acrylic/25 per cent wool) from Plymouth Yarn Co.

SOCK HOP

Knit socks will make your feet feel like dancing!

Design by Patsy Leatherbury

Skill Level
INTERMEDIATE

Size
Woman's medium

Finished Measurements
Top: Approx 6½ inches to top of heel
Circumference: Approx 7 inches

Materials

Sock weight yarn (215 yds/2 oz per skein):
   2 skeins orange/pink
Size 2 (2.75mm) double-pointed needles or size
   needed to obtain gauge
Stitch marker

Gauge
15 sts = 2 inches/5cm in St st
To save time, take time to check gauge.

Cuff
Cast on 96 sts. Arrange sts on 3 needles with 32 sts on each needle. Mark beg of rnd.

Rnd 1: *K2tog, p2tog; rep from * around. (48 sts)

Rnds 2–11: *K1, p1; rep from * around.

Leg
Begin pat
Rnds 1 and 2: Knit around.

Rnd 3: Purl around.

Rnds 4–6: Rep Rnds 1–3.

Rnds 7–10: Knit around.

Rnd 11: *K1, yo, k3, pass 3rd st on RH needle over first 2 sts; rep from * around.

Rnds 12–14: Knit around.

Rnd 15: K3, *yo, ssk, k6; rep from * to last 5 sts, end yo, ssk, k3.

Rnds 16, 18, 20 and 22: Knit around.

Rnd 17: K2, *[yo, ssk] twice, k4; rep from * to last 6 sts, end [yo, ssk] twice, k2.

Rnd 19: K1, *[yo, ssk] 3 times, k2; rep from * to last 7 sts, end [yo, ssk] 3 times, k1.

Rnd 21: K2, *[yo, ssk] twice, k4; rep from * to last 6 sts, end [yo, ssk] twice, k2.

Sock Hop
Sample project was knit with Shepherd Sock (80 per cent wool/20 per cent nylon) from Lorna's Laces.

Rnd 23: K3, *yo, ssk, k6; rep from * to last 5 sts, end yo, ssk, k3.

Rnds 24–26: Knit around.

Rnd 27: *K1, yo, k3, pass 3rd st on RH needle over first 2 sts; rep from * around.

Rnds 28–31: Knit around.

Rnd 32: Purl around.

Rnds 33 and 34: Knit around.

Rnd 35: Purl around.

Rnds 36–48: Knit around.

Heel flap

Arrange sts with 10 sts on needle 1, 28 sts on needle 2, and 10 sts on needle 3.

With 3rd needle, knit across 10 sts of first needle, turn. Heel flap will be worked in rows on these 20 sts only.

Notes: You may wish to divide instep sts between 2 needles to make it easier to work. On heel flap, sl sts purlwise.

Next row: Sl 1, p19.

Row 1: *Sl 1, k1; rep from * across.

Row 2: Sl 1, purl across.

Row 3: Sl 1, *sl 1, k1; rep from * to last st, k1.

Row 4: Sl 1, purl across.

Rows 5–20: [Rep Rows 1–4] 4 more times. (20 rows of heel flap st total)

Turn heel

Row 1: Sl 1, k10, ssk, k1, turn.

Row 2: Sl 1, p3, p2tog, p1, turn.

Row 3: Sl 1, knit to last st before gap, ssk, k1, turn.

Row 4: Sl 1, purl to last st before gap, p2tog, p1, turn.

Rep Rows 3 and 4 until all sts are worked. (12 sts)

Gusset

Knit across 12 heel sts, with same needle, pick up and knit 12 sts along edge of heel flap; with needle 2, knit across 28 instep sts; with needle 3, pick up and knit 12 sts along edge of heel flap, then with same needle knit first 6 sts from needle 1. (sts are divided 18-28-18)

Knit 1 rnd.

Rnd 1: On needle 1, knit to last 3 sts, k2tog, k1; on needle 2, knit across; on needle 3, k1, ssk, knit to end.

Rnd 2: Knit around.

Rep Rnds 1 and 2 until first and 3rd needles have 10 sts each, ending with Rnd 2. (48 sts rem)

Foot

Divide sts with 12 sts each on needles 1 and 3, 24 instep sts on needle 2.

Knit 48 rnds or until foot measures 2 inches less than desired length.

Shape toe

Rnd 1: On needle 1, knit to last 3 sts, ssk, k1; on needle 2, k1, k2tog, knit to last 3 sts, ssk, k1; on needle 3, k1, k2tog, knit to end.

Rnd 2: Knit around.

Rep Rnds 1 and 2 until 28 sts rem, ending with Rnd 2, then [rep Rnd 1] 3 times. (16 sts rem)

With needle 3, knit across sts from needle 1. Cut yarn, leaving a 16-inch tail. (8 sts each on 2 needles)

With tapestry needle, weave toe referring to Kitchener Stitch (see page 24). ■

SEND A LITTLE CABLE

Keep winter's chill away in style— no cable needle required!

Design by Amy Polcyn

Skill Level

INTERMEDIATE

Size
Adult

Finished Measurement
Foot circumference: 8 inches

Materials
Worsted weight yarn (100 yds/50g per ball):
  2 balls red
Size 6 (4mm) double-pointed needles or size
  needed to obtain gauge
Stitch holder
Tapestry needle

MEDIUM

Gauge
20 sts and 28 rows = 4 inches/10cm in pat
To save time, take time to check gauge.

Pattern Stitch
Baby Cable (multiple of 4 sts)

Rnds 1–3: *K2, p2; rep from * around.

Rnd 4: *K2tog, leave on LH needle, insert tip of RH needle back into first st, k1, sl sts off needle, p2; rep from * around.

Rep Rnds 1–4 for pat.

Pattern Note
Slip all stitches purlwise.

Leg
Cast on 40 sts, divide evenly on dpns and join without twisting. Work in Baby Cable pat for 4 inches, ending with Rnd 4 of pat.

Heel Flap
K8, turn. P18. These sts will form heel flap. Place rem 22 instep sts on holder. Heel flap is worked back and forth in rows.

Row 1: *Sl 1, k1; rep from * across.

Row 2: Sl 1, purl across.

Rows 3–18: Rep Rows 1 and 2.

There will be 9 chain selvedge sts along each side of heel flap.

Turn Heel
Row 1: K11, ssk, k1, turn.

Row 2: Sl 1, p5, p2tog, p1, turn.

Send a Little Cable
Sample project was knit with Karaoke (50 per cent soy silk/50 per cent wool) from South West Trading Co.

Row 3: Sl 1, knit to 1 st before gap, ssk (taking 1 st from each side of gap), k1, turn.

Row 4: Sl 1, purl to 1 st before gap, p2tog (taking 1 st from each side of gap), p1, turn.

Rep Rows 3 and 4 until all heel sts have been worked, ending with a WS row. (12 sts)

Gusset

Knit across 12 heel sts and pick up and knit 9 sts along side of heel flap (needle 1), work 22 instep sts in pat (needle 2); pick up and knit 9 sts along other side of heel flap (needle 3); knit across half of heel sts (6 sts) and mark centre back heel as beg of rnd. (52 sts)

Rnd 1: Knit to last 3 sts on needle 1, k2tog, k1; work instep sts in pat on needle 2; on needle 3, k1, ssk, knit to end.

Rnd 2: Work even in established pats.

Rep Rnds 1 and 2 until 40 sts rem.

Foot

Rep Rnd 2 until foot measures approximately 2 inches less than desired length.

Toe

Note: Discontinue pat and work all sts in St st.

Rnd 1: Knit to last 3 sts on needle 1, k2tog, k1; on needle 2, k1, ssk, knit to last 3 sts, k2tog, k1; on needle 3, work k1, ssk, knit to end.

Rnd 2: Knit around.

Rep Rnds 1 and 2 until 8 sts rem. Divide sts evenly between 2 needles. With tapestry needle, weave toe, referring to Kitchener Stitch (see page 24). ∎

PRETTY STRIPE SOCKS

*Peppermint or cotton candy stripes
are great for sweet feet.*

Designs by Patsy J. Leatherbury

Peppermint

Skill Level
INTERMEDIATE

Size
Woman's medium

Materials
Light weight yarn (100 yds/50g per ball):
 1 ball each red MC) and white (CC)
Size 2 (2.75mm) set of 4 double-pointed needles
 or size needed to obtain gauge

Gauge
12 sts and 18 rnds = 2 inches/5cm in St st in rnds
To save time, take time to check gauge.

Cuff
With MC, cast on 80 sts. Divide sts among 3 needles with
20 sts each on needles 1 and 3, and 40 sts on needle 2.
Join without twisting.

Rnds 1 and 2: *K2, p2; rep from * around.

Rnd 3: *K2tog, p2tog; rep from * around. (40 sts)

Leg
Rnds 4–7: *K1, p1; rep from * around. Change to CC.

Rnds 8–11: Rep Rnds 4–7. Change to MC.

Rnds 12–15: Rep Rnds 4–7. Change to CC.

Rnds 16–31: [Rep Rnds 8–15] twice.

Rnds 32 and 33: With CC, knit around. Fasten off CC,
change to MC.

Heel flap
With MC only, with needle 3, knit across needle 1, turn
work. Sts are on 2 needles with 20 sts on each needle.
Heel flap will be worked on 20 sts of back needle only.

*Note: For ease in working you may wish to divide instep
sts between 2 needles.*

Next row (WS): Sl 1, p19.

Row 1: *Sl 1, k1; rep from * across, end with k1, turn.

Row 2: Sl 1, purl across, turn.

Row 3: Sl 1, *sl 1, k1; rep from * to last st, k1, turn.

Row 4: Sl 1, purl across, turn.

Rows 5–24: [Rep Rows 1–4] 5 more times.

Turn heel

Row 1: Sl 1, k10, ssk, k1, turn, leaving 6 sts unworked.

Row 2: Sl 1, p3, p2tog, p1, turn, leaving 6 sts unworked.

Row 3: Sl 1, knit to last st before gap, ssk, k1, turn.

Row 4: Sl 1, purl to last st before gap, p2tog, p1, turn.

Rep Rows 3 and 4 until all sts are worked. (12 sts)

Gussets

Knit across 12 heel sts on needle, with same needle, pick up and knit 14 sts along edge of heel flap; with 2nd needle, knit across 20 instep sts; with 3rd needle, pick up and knit 14 sts along edge of heel flap, then with same needle, knit first 6 sts from first needle. (60 sts; 20 sts on each of 3 needles)

Work 1 rnd of St st. Attach CC.

Rnd 1: With CC, knit to last 3 sts on first needle, k2tog, k1, knit even across 2nd needle; on 3rd needle, k1, ssk, knit to end of needle.

Rnd 2: Knit around. Change to MC yarn.

Rep Rnds 1 and 2, changing colours every 2 rnds until 40 sts rem. (10 sts each on needles 1 and 3, 20 sts on needle 2)

Foot

Continuing to alternate colours every 2 rnds, work even until foot measures approx 6½ inches, or 1–2 inches less than desired length, ending with 2nd rnd of either colour. Fasten off CC, continue to work with MC only.

Shape toe

With needle 3, knit across needle 1. Sts are on 2 needles with 20 sts on front needle and 20 sts back needle.

Rnd 1: On front needle, k1, ssk, knit to last 3 sts, k2tog, k1; rep for back needle.

Rnd 2: Knit around.

Rep Rnds 1 and 2 until 12 sts rem on each needle, ending with Rnd 1.

[Rep Rnd 1] twice more, leaving 8 sts on each needle.

With tapestry needle, weave toe, referring to Kitchener Stitch (see page 24).

Cotton Candy

Skill Level
INTERMEDIATE

Size
Woman's medium

Materials
Light weight yarn (100 yds/50g per ball):
   1 ball each pink (MC) and white (CC)
Size 2 (2.75mm) set of 4 double-pointed needles
   or size needed to obtain gauge

Gauge
12 sts and 18 rnds = 2 inches/5cm in St st in rnds
To save time, take time to check gauge.

Cuff
With MC, cast on 80 sts. Divide sts among 3 needles with

20 sts each on needles 1 and 3, and 40 sts on needle 2. Join without twisting.

Rnds 1 and 2: *K2, p2; rep from * around.

Rnd 3: *K2tog, p2tog; rep from * around. (40 sts)

Leg

Rnds 4–9: *K1, p1; rep from * around. Change to CC.

Rnds 10–15: Rep Rnds 4–9 with CC. Change to MC.

Rnds 16 and 17: *K1, p1; rep from * around. Change to CC.

Rnds 18–23: *K1, p1; rep from * around. Change to MC.

Rnds 24–29: Rep Rnds 4–9 with MC. Change to CC.

Rnds 30 and 31: With CC, knit around.

Change to MC, fasten off CC and complete heel, foot and toe as for Peppermint Sock. ■

Pretty Stripe Socks
Sample projects were knit with Fixation #3628, #8001 and #3077 (98.3 per cent cotton/1.7 per cent elastic) from Cascade Yarns

CURVY LACE SOCKS

*Feel like you are walking on air
in these special socks.*

Design by Kathy Wesley

Skill Level

■■■☐ INTERMEDIATE

Size
Woman's medium

Materials
Sport weight yarn (136 yds/50g per ball):
  2 balls mango
Size 3 (3.25mm) double-pointed needles or size
  needed to obtain gauge
Stitch holder
Stitch markers

Gauge
14 sts = 2 inches/5cm in St st
To save time, take time to check gauge.

Special Abbreviation
M1 (Make 1): Inc 1 by picking up horizontal lp between
the last st worked and the next st and knitting in back
of this lp.

Pattern Stitches
Curvy Lace (for cuff; multiple of 9 sts)

Rnd 1 (RS): Knit.

Rnd 2 and all even-numbered rnds: *P2, k7; rep from
* around.

Rnd 3: *K3, yo, k2, ssk, k2; rep from * around.

Rnd 5: *K4, yo, k2, ssk, k1; rep from * around.

Rnd 7: *K5, yo, k2, ssk; rep from * around.

Rnd 9: Knit.

Rnd 11: *K4, k2tog, k2, yo, k1; rep from * around.

Rnd 13: *K3, k2tog, k2, yo, k2; rep from * around.

Rnd 15: *K2, k2tog, k2, yo, k3; rep from * around.

Rnd 16: *P2, k7; rep from * around.

Rep Rnds 1–16 for pat.

Instep (panel of 24 sts)

Rnd 1: Knit.

Rnd 2 and all even-numbered rnds: K2, [p2, k7] twice,
p2, k2.

Rnd 3: K2, [k3, yo, k2, ssk, k2] twice, k4.

Rnd 5: K2, [k4, yo, k2, ssk, k1] twice, k4.

Curvy Lace Socks
Sample project was knit with Grace (100 per cent mercerized cotton) from Patons.

Rnd 7: K2, [k5, yo, k2, ssk] twice, k4.

Rnd 9: Knit.

Rnd 11: K2, [k4, k2tog, k2, yo, k1] twice, k4.

Rnd 13: K2, [k3, k2tog, k2, yo, k2] twice, k4.

Rnd 15: K2, [k2, k2tog, k2, yo, k3] twice, k4.

Rnd 16: K2, [p2, k7] twice, p2, k2.

Rep Rnds 1–16 for pat.

Pattern Note

Charts are provided for the pattern stitch used for cuff and instep of sock. When working from chart on double-pointed needles in the round, all rounds are right side rounds and are read on the chart from right to left.

Cuff

Cast on 52 sts. Divide sts onto 3 needles, having 17 sts on first needle, 18 sts on 2nd needle and 17 sts on 3rd needle. Join without twisting.

Rnd 1: *K2, p2; rep from * around.

Rep Rnd 1 until piece measures 1½ inches.

Next rnd: Continuing in k2, p2 rib, inc 2 sts (by M1) evenly spaced. (54 sts)

Leg

Work [Rnds 1–16 of Curvy Lace pat] twice.

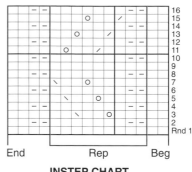

INSTEP CHART

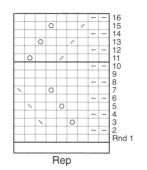

CUFF CHART

STITCH KEY
☐ K on RS
– P on RS
○ Yo
╱ K2tog
╲ Ssk

Heel

Sl last 12 sts of last rnd onto free needle. Knit first 14 sts on next needle onto same needle. (26 sts for heel)

Sl rem 28 sts to holder for instep.

Heel flap

Row 1 (WS): P1, p2tog, purl to last 3 sts, p2tog, p1. (24 sts)

Row 2: Sl 1k, knit across. Turn.

Row 3: Sl 1p, purl across. Turn.

Rows 4–21: [Rep Rows 2 and 3] 9 times more.

Row 22: Rep Row 2.

Turn heel
Row 1 (WS): P14, p2tog, p1, turn, leaving rem 7 sts unworked.

Row 2: Sl 1k, k5, ssk, k1, turn, leaving rem 7 sts unworked.

Row 3: Sl 1p, p6, p2tog, p1, turn, leaving rem 5 sts unworked.

Row 4: Sl 1k, k7, ssk, k1, turn, leaving rem 5 sts unworked.

Row 5: Sl 1p, p8, p2tog, p1, turn, leaving rem 3 sts unworked.

Row 6: Sl 1k, k9, ssk, k1, turn, leaving rem 3 sts unworked.

Row 7: Sl 1p, p10, p2tog, p1, turn, leaving rem st unworked.

Row 8: Sl 1k, k11, ssk, k1, turn, leaving rem st unworked.

Row 9: Sl 1p, p12, p2tog, turn.

Row 10: Sl 1k, k12, ssk. (14 sts)

Gusset
Place instep sts on free needle.

Rnd 1: Sl last 7 sts of heel to free needle, on same needle pick up and knit 13 sts along side of heel, knit 2 sts from instep needle; work Rnd 1 of Instep pat (or chart) across next 24 instep sts; knit 2 rem instep sts onto free needle, with same needle pick up and knit 13 sts along other side of heel, knit 7 rem heel sts. (68 sts)

Rnd 2: On first needle, knit to last 3 sts, k2tog, k1; on 2nd needle work Rnd 2 of Instep pat; on 3rd needle k1, ssk, knit rem sts. (66 sts)

Rnd 3: On first needle, knit; on 2nd needle work Rnd 3 of Instep pat; on 3rd needle, knit.

Continue in established Instep pat on 2nd needle and dec 1 st at end of first needle and beg of 3rd needle as above [every other row] 9 times. (48 sts).

Work even, maintaining Instep pat on 2nd needle until foot is about 2 inches less than desired length.

Toe
Note: All rnds are knit.

Rnd 1: On first needle, knit to last 3 sts, k2tog, k1; on 2nd needle, k1, ssk, knit to last 3 sts, k2tog, k1; on 3rd needle, k1, ssk, knit rem sts.

Rnd 2: Knit.

Rnds 3–12: [Rep Rnds 1 and 2] 5 times more. (24 sts)

Rnds 13 and 14: Rep Rnd 1. (16 sts)

Knit sts from first needle onto 3rd needle. Cut yarn, leaving a 12-inch end for weaving.

Finishing
With tapestry needle, weave toe referring to Kitchener Stitch (see page 24). ∎

CRISSCROSS CABLE GLASS COZY

This knit-in-the-round cozy will stretch to fit your glass or a water bottle.

Design by Kathy Wesley

Skill Level

EASY

Size

Fits glass or bottle with up to 9½ inch circumference

Materials

Sport weight yarn (150 yds/43g per ball):
   1 ball lime
Size 2 (2.75mm) double-pointed needles
Cable needle
Stitch marker

Gauge

16 sts = 2 inches/5cm in pat (slightly stretched)
Exact gauge is not critical to this project.

Special Abbreviation

CB (Cable Back): Sl next 2 sts to cn and hold in back, k2, k2 from cn.

Ribbing

Beg at top, cast 60 sts onto 1 needle. Divide evenly onto 3 needles, join without twisting, mark beg of rnd.

Rnd 1: *P2, k2; rep from * around.

Rep Rnd 1 until ribbing measures 1 inch.

Body

Begin pat

Rnds 1–4: *P1, k4, p2, k2, p1; rep from * around.

Rnd 5: P1, CB, p2, k2, p1; rep from * around.

Rnds 6–8: Rep Rnd 1.

Rnds 9–12: *P2, k2, p2, k4; rep from * around.

Rnd 13: *P2, k2, p2, CB; rep from * around.

Rnds 14–16: Rep Rnd 9.

[Rep Rnds 1–16] twice.

Shape bottom

Rnd 1: [K8, k2tog] 6 times. (54 sts)

Rnd 2: [K7, k2tog] 6 times. (48 sts)

Rnd 3: [K6, k2tog] 6 times. (42 sts)

Rnd 4: [K5, k2tog] 6 times. (36 sts)

Rnd 5: [K4, k2tog] 6 times. (30 sts)

Rnd 6: [K3, k2tog] 6 times. (24 sts)

Crisscross Cable Glass Cozy
Sample project was knit with Senso Microfiber Cotton (60 per cent cotton/40 per cent acrylic) from DMC.

Rnd 7: [K2, k2tog] 6 times. (18 sts)

Rnd 8: [K1, k2tog] 6 times. (12 sts)

Rnd 9: [K2tog] 6 times. (6 sts)

Cut yarn, leaving a long end.

Weave end through rem sts and fasten securely. ∎

JUST-FOR-HER STOCKING

This especially sweet stocking design will be a joy to hang every year!

Design by Kathleen Power Johnson

Skill Level ◐■☐▢
EASY

Size
Approx 16 inches long

Materials
Worsted weight yarn (200 yds/4 oz per skein):
   1 skein Irish green (MC)
Worsted weight yarn (128 yds/100g per skein):
   1 skein red (CC)
Size 8 (5mm) set of 4 double-pointed needles or size
   needed to obtain gauge
Stitch holders
Stitch marker
Size E/4 (3.5mm) crochet hook
#3 pearl cotton: 1 skein red
¾ yd ⅜-inch-wide ribbon
Sewing needle and matching thread

Gauge
17 sts and 27 rows = 4 inches/10cm in St st
To save time, take time to check gauge.

Pattern Note
Slip all stitches purlwise.

Cuff
With MC, cast on 54 sts. Divide sts evenly onto 3 needles.
Mark beg of rnd.

Rnd 1: Knit.

Rnd 2: Purl.

Rnds 3–8: [Rep Rnds 1 and 2] 3 times.

Rnds 9–14: Knit.

Body
Rnd 1: *K3, p1, k2; rep from * around.

Rnd 2: *K2, [p1, k1] twice, rep from * around.

Rnd 3: *K1, p1, k3, p1; rep from * around.

Rnd 4: *P1, k5; rep from * around.

Rnd 5: Rep Rnd 3.

Rnd 6: Rep Rnd 2.

[Rep Rnds 1–6] 7 times more.

Next rnd: Knit. Cut MC.

Heel Flap
Sl 18 sts from first needle onto holder for instep. With CC, knit 18 sts from 2nd needle and 8 sts from 3rd needle.

Just-for-Her Stocking

Sample project was knit with
Matisse (100 per cent wool)
from Rainbow Mills, Manos
(100 per cent wool) from Manos
de Uruguay, and pearl cotton
from DMC.

Place rem 10 sts from 3rd needle onto another holder for instep, turn. (26 sts on needle, 28 sts on holders)

Row 1 (WS): Sl 1, [k1, p1] 12 times, k1.

Row 2: Sl 1, [p1, k1] 12 times, p1.

Rows 3–14: [Rep Rows 1 and 2] 6 times.

Row 15: Rep Row 1.

Turn Heel
Row 1 (RS): Sl 1, k13, ssk, k1.

Row 2: Sl 1, p3, p2tog, p1.

Row 3: Sl 1, k4, ssk, k1.

Row 4: Sl 1, p5, p2tog, p1.

Row 5: Sl 1, k6, ssk, k1.

Row 6: Sl 1, p7, p2tog, p1.

Row 7: Sl 1, k8, ssk, k1.

Row 8: Sl 1, p9, p2tog, p1.

Row 9: Sl 1, k10, ssk, k1.

Row 10: Sl 1, p11, p2tog, p1.

Row 11: Sl 1, k12, ssk.

Row 12: Sl 1, p12, p2tog.

Row 13: Knit. (14 sts)

Cut CC and join MC.

Gusset
Hold heel with RS facing, on same needle, pick up and knit 8 sts along side of heel flap; k18 sts from holder and 10 sts from 2nd holder onto 2nd needle (instep); with 3rd needle pick up and knit 8 sts along side of heel flap, k7 sts from first needle onto 3rd needle. Sl 1 st from end of 2nd needle to first needle, and 1 st from other end of 2nd needle to 3rd needle. Mark beg of rnd. (58 sts)

Rnd 1: On first needle knit to last 4 sts, k2tog, k2; on 2nd needle knit across; on 3rd needle k2, ssk, knit to end. (56 sts)

Rnd 2: Knit.

Rnds 3–6: [Rep Rnds 1 and 2] twice. (52 sts)

Foot
Rnd 1: Purl.

Rnd 2: Knit.

Rnds 3 and 4: Rep Rnds 1 and 2.

Rnds 5–10: Knit.

Rnds 11–14: [Rep Rnds 1 and 2] twice. Cut MC.

Toe
Join CC.

Rnd 1: Knit.

Rnd 2: On first needle, knit to last 3 sts, k2tog, k1; on 2nd needle, k1, ssk, knit to last 3 sts, k2tog, k1; on 3rd needle, k1, ssk, knit rem sts. (48 sts)

Rnds 3–6: [Rep Rnds 1 and 2] twice. (40 sts)

Rnds 7–13: [Rep Rnd 2] 6 times more. (16 sts)

Divide sts onto 2 needles by working sts from needle 3 onto needle 1. Cut yarn, leaving a 12-inch end for weaving.

Trim

With pearl cotton make slip knot on hook and join with a sc in last purl row of garter st cuff, sc in next st, *ch 3, sl st in last sc made, sc in next 4 sts; rep from * around, join in first sc. Finish off.

Referring to photo for placement, work trim in same manner on 3 garter st ridges on foot.

Finishing

With tapestry needle and end, weave toe tog, referring to Kitchener Stitch (see page 24).

Cut 6 (3-inch) lengths of ribbon and tie in bows. Sew as desired to top of stocking. Use rem ribbon for hanging lp. ■

Crochet Basics

Chain Stitch (ch)

Begin by making a slip knot on the hook. Bring the yarn over the hook from back to front and draw through the loop on the hook.

Chain Stitch

For each additional chain stitch, bring the yarn over the hook from back to front and draw through the loop on the hook.

Single Crochet (sc)

Insert the hook in the second chain through the centre of the V. Bring the yarn over the hook from back to front.

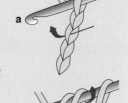

a

Draw the yarn through the chain stitch and onto the hook.

b

Again bring yarn over the hook from back to front and draw it through both loops on hook.

c

For additional rows of single crochet, insert the hook under both loops of the previous stitch instead of through the centre of the V as when working into the chain stitch.

SLUMBER PARTY SLEEPING BAG

Knitting an afghan in the round transforms it into a delightful child's sleeping bag.

Design by Jacqueline Hoyle

Skill Level

INTERMEDIATE

Sizes

48 (50, 51, 53) x 48 (48, 57, 57) inches Instructions are given for smallest size, with larger sizes in parentheses. When only 1 number is given, it applies to all sizes.

Materials

Chunky weight yarn (143 yds/100g per skein):
  8 (8, 9, 9) skeins aqua (A) and 3 balls
  chartreuse (B)
DK weight yarn (126 yds/50g per ball):
  1 (1, 2, 2) balls white (C)
Novelty eyelash yarn (190 yds/50g per ball):
  1 ball lavender (D)
Size 15 (10mm) double-pointed needles (2 only)
  and 36-inch circular needle or size needed to obtain
  gauge
Stitch marker
Stitch holder
Tapestry needle

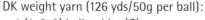

Gauge

16 sts and 27 rows = 4 inches/10cm in triple-slip st pat
15 sts and 16 rows = 4 inches/10cm in Three Flower pat
To save time, take time to check gauge.

Special Abbreviations

CD: Hold 1 strand each of C and D tog.

MB (Make Bobble): P3, turn, k3, turn, sl 1, k2tog, psso.

Pattern Stitch

Three Flowers (multiple of 10 sts)

Rnds 1–4: With A, knit.

Rnd 5: With B, knit.

Rnd 6: With B, *p3 wrapping yarn 3 times for each st, p7; rep from * around.

Rnd 7: With A, *sl 3 wyib dropping extra wraps, k3, sl 1 wyib, k3; rep from * around.

Rnd 8: With A, *sl 3 wyib, k3, sl 1 wyib, k3; rep from * around.

Rnds 9 and 10: With A, *sl 3 wyib, k7; rep from * around.

Rnd 11: With A, sl 1 B wyib, *k1 B, drop next B st off needle to front of work, k2, place dropped st back on LH needle and knit it, k3, sl 2 wyib, drop next B st off needle to front of work, place 2 sl sts back on LH needle, pick up dropped st and knit it, k2; rep from *, end last rep sl 2 wyib, drop B off LH needle, sl 2 sts back onto LH needle, place dropped st on LH needle, k3.

Slumber Party Sleeping Bag

Sample project was knit with Encore Chunky (75 per cent acrylic/25 per cent wool), Dreambaby Kokonut DK (67 per cent microfiber acrylic/33 per cent nylon) and Flash (100 per cent nylon) from Plymouth Yarn Co.

Rnd 12: With CD, *(k1, p1, k1) in next st, sl 2 wyib, (k1, p1, k1) in next st, sl 3 wyib, (k1, p1, k1) in next st, sl 2 wyib; rep from *, end last rep (k1, p1, k1) in next st, sl 2 wyib.

Rnd 13: With CD, *MB, sl 2 wyib, MB, sl 3 wyib, *[MB, sl 2 wyib] twice, MB, sl 3 wyib; rep from *, end last rep MB, sl 2 wyib.

Rnd 14: With A, knit, working each bobble tbl.

Rnds 15–18: Rep Rnds 1–4.

Pattern Notes
One strand each of C and D are always held together.

When working in the round, read all rounds from right to left, working area between red lines only.

When working in rows, all odd-numbered rows are right side rows. Work complete chart, including selvage stitches.

To prevent long float on Rounds 10 and 20 of chart, work as follows: with yarn in front, carry yarn across 3 stitches at end of row, slip marker, slip first stitch of new row to right-hand needle, with yarn in back place same stitch back on left-hand needle; with yarn in front slip 3 stitches to right-hand needle and continue in pattern across row.

Sleeping Bag
With A, cast on 180 (186, 192, 198) sts. Join without twisting, place marker between first and last st.

*[Work Rnds 1–20 of chart] twice.

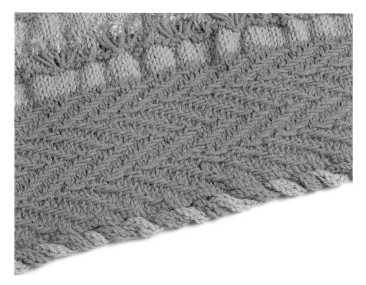

Work Rnds 1–18 of Three Flowers pat, dec 0 (6, 2, 8) sts on first rnd and inc 0 (6, 2, 8) sts on last rnd; rep from * 3 (3, 4, 4) times. Bag will measure approx 41 (41, 51, 51) inches.

Top Flaps
Work in rows from this point.

Row 1: With B, k90 (93, 96, 99) sts, inc 5 (2, 5, 2) sts evenly. Place rem sts on holder. (95, 95, 101, 101 sts)

Keeping first and last st in St st for selvage, work even from chart until 40 rows have been completed.

Work in garter st for 3 rows, inc (inc, dec, dec) 5 (5, 1, 1) sts on first row. (100 sts)

Knit 1 row, place sts on holder.

Sl st from first holder to needle. Work 2nd flap the same.

Border Triangles
Make 10

With colour of your choice, cast on 2 sts.

Next row: *Yo, knit to end of row.

Rep this row until there are 20 sts on needle.

Place sts on holder.

Finishing
Place 5 triangles on 1 needle; place sts of 1 top flap on 2nd needle.

Holding needles parallel, k2tog (1 st from each needle) across row.

Bind off.

Rep for 2nd side.

Tack triangles to outside of bag.

I-Cord Trim
With A, cast on 3 sts.

*K3, sl sts back to LH needle; rep from * until cord measures 1½ times the width of bottom of bag. Place sts on holder.

With B, make 2nd cord the same.

Finishing
Twist cords tog loosely and pin to bottom edge of bag, adjusting length of cords if necessary.

Bind off and sew in place. ■

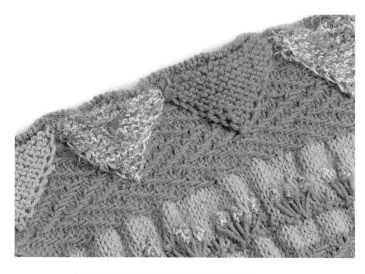

STITCH KEY
☐ K on RS, p on WS
⊟ Sl 1 wyif on RS, sl 1 wyib on WS.

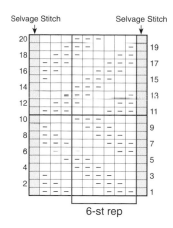

Selvage Stitch   Selvage Stitch

6-st rep

INDEX

Sweaters & Wraps

Dot & Dash Pullover, 40

Babies & Kids

Little Miss Precious, 64   Shades for Play, 70

INDEX

Hats & Mittens

School Colours
Scarf & Hat, 78

Rolled-Brim Hat & Mitts, 81

Jacquard Hat & Glittens, 93

Quick Unisex Hats, 84

Sweetheart Hat, 90

Berets for Mom &
Daughter, 87

Silly Hat, 97

Socks & Sundry

Send a Little Cable, 104

Crisscross Cable Glass
Cozy, 114

Just-for-Her Stocking, 116

Sock Hop, 100

Curvy Lace Socks, 110

Pretty Stripe Socks, 107

Slumber Party Sleeping Bag, 120

GENERAL INFORMATION

Metric Conversion Charts

METRIC CONVERSIONS

yards	x	.9144	=	metres (m)
yards	x	91.44	=	centimetres (cm)
inches	x	2.54	=	centimetres (cm)
inches	x	25.40	=	millimetres (mm)
inches	x	.0254	=	metres (m)

centimetres	x	.3937	=	inches
metres	x	1.0936	=	yards

INCHES INTO MILLIMETRES & CENTIMETRES (Rounded off slightly)

inches	mm	cm	inches	cm	inches	cm	inches	cm
1/8	3	0.3	5	12.5	21	53.5	38	96.5
1/4	6	0.6	5 1/2	14	22	56	39	99
3/8	10	1	6	15	23	58.5	40	101.5
1/2	13	1.3	7	18	24	61	41	104
5/8	15	1.5	8	20.5	25	63.5	42	106.5
3/4	20	2	9	23	26	66	43	109
7/8	22	2.2	10	25.5	27	68.5	44	112
1	25	2.5	11	28	28	71	45	114.5
1 1/4	32	3.2	12	30.5	29	73.5	46	117
1 1/2	38	3.8	13	33	30	76	47	119.5
1 3/4	45	4.5	14	35.5	31	79	48	122
2	50	5	15	38	32	81.5	49	124.5
2 1/2	65	6.5	16	40.5	33	84	50	127
3	75	7.5	17	43	34	86.5		
3 1/2	90	9	18	46	35	89		
4	100	10	19	48.5	36	91.5		
4 1/2	115	11.5	20	51	37	94		

KNITTING NEEDLES CONVERSION CHART

Canada/U.S.	0	1	2	3	4	5	6	7	8	9	10	10½	11	13	15
Metric (mm)	2	2¼	2¾	3¼	3½	3¾	4	4½	5	5½	6	6½	8	9	10

CROCHET HOOKS CONVERSION CHART

Canada/U.S.	1/B	2/C	3/D	4/E	5/F	6/G	8/H	9/I	10/J	10½/K	N
Metric (mm)	2.25	2.75	3.25	3.5	3.75	4.25	5	5.5	6	6.5	9.0

Skill Levels

BEGINNER

Projects for first-time knitters using basic knit and purl stitches. Minimal shaping.

EASY

Projects using basic stitches, repetitive stitch patterns, simple colour changes and simple shaping and finishing.

INTERMEDIATE

Projects with a variety of stitches, such as basic cables and lace, simple intarsia, double-pointed needles and knitting in the round needle techniques, mid-level shaping and finishing.

EXPERIENCED

Projects using advanced techniques and stitches, such as short rows, Fair Isle, more intricate intarsia, cables, lace patterns and numerous colour changes.

Our website is filled with
all kinds of great information
www.companyscoming.com

More than 25 years
and more than 25 million
cookbooks sold—that's quite a
feat. Now we're giving you the same attention
to detail in our new craft books as we always have in our
cookbooks—lots of great photos, easy-to-follow instructions
and choices galore! It's time to get a little crafty with us!

Company's
Coming